D1648963

GOD IS
FOR US

C. BAXTER KRUGER, Ph.D.

Perichoresis Press

www.perichoresis.org

To
David Upshaw, Clayton James and Steve Horn
in the hope of 2 Corinthians 5:19

CONTENTS

Foreword

This beautifully written book reads like a hymn of praise to the Triune God of grace, who has created and redeemed this world to fulfill His purposes of glory. It is written with a passionate desire to communicate profound biblical theology in simple contemporary language, that the Church might always be faithful to her true center in Jesus Christ.

God is love, and love always implies communion between persons, and that is what we see in God Himself and in His purposes for this world. The Father loves the Son in the communion of the Spirit, and the Son loves the Father in the communion of the Spirit, in their mutual 'indwelling,' *perichoresis*.

It is this Triune God of grace who created this world to be 'the theatre of His glory,' and us, as men and women, to participate in the very life of God, that we too might find our true being in intimate loving communion with Him and one another. These glorious purposes are brought to fulfillment for us and in us by Jesus Christ, who draws us by the Spirit into the very life of God. It is in these terms that Dr. Kruger expounds the central doctrines of the faith so lucidly—the incarnation, vicarious humanity, substitutionary atonement and continuing priesthood of our Lord.

James B. Torrance, Professor Emeritus
Kings College, University of Aberdeen

Chapter 1 - The Eternal Gospel of the Father

Ephesians 1:3-6

The apostle Paul begins his great letter to the Ephesians with a burst of praise: "*Blessed* be the God and Father of our Lord Jesus Christ, who has blessed us with every spiritual blessing in the heavenly places in Christ Jesus." Here is no bored old man trying to muster a tired bit of religious liturgy. This is an *outburst* of genuine praise that comes from excitement over glimpsing what God has done with us in Christ.

This man has seen that something quite breathtaking and glorious has taken place in Jesus Christ and that it involves *us*—you, me, the world.

He has seen the sovereign grace of the Father overflow and lavish upon us an almost indescribable heavenly gift in Christ. And, as we read further, we cannot help but feel that the apostle will explode if he does not get it out. He rattles on for ten or so verses without taking a breath.

Can you not feel the apostle's heart here? Awesome things have happened in Christ. We are included. They are for us and involve us. And the apostle is bursting at the seams to help us see it all with him. He strains word after word and stretches phrase after phrase, almost to the breaking point, as if what he sees is beyond words or expression.

But he must express it. He is driven to put it before us. He is a desperately inspired man. He feels that if he can communicate here all history will be changed.

The question is: What is it that has the apostle so energized to communicate? What is it that he sees and feels? What is it that has gotten such a hold on this man? We would do well to focus all our attention on these questions.

There are three key points. But before we probe these points, we need to understand that Paul is taking it for granted that we all know that this is God's world. There is a God. And this God created everything in the heavens and on earth. What the apostle is on about here is *why* God created the world and humanity. He is con-

1

cerned to explain the rhyme and reason of God's creative activity and thus our very existence.

The first point that Paul is making is that God the Father has a plan, an eternal plan, formulated, as it were, before anything was ever created, and standing as the secret behind all things. Second, the Father has not left the execution of His plan to chance—or to kings and governments, the church and politics, or to you and me. He has appointed an executor of His will. He has designated One to accomplish His purpose. He has placed One in charge of working out His plan to the full. Third, this plan has now been fulfilled.

Paul is not trading in theoretical abstractions. He is not talking about what may happen at some later time when *we* finally get things straightened out. God forbid! The apostle sees that God's plan has an astonishing surprise in it. The Father has appointed His Son to step forth and work out His eternal purpose. And Paul is standing in awe because this is what has happened. Jesus has come. The work is finished. What the Father planned for us before creation has now been decisively fulfilled in Jesus Christ.

This first chapter of Ephesians is the apostle's verbal attempt to grab us and shake us and wake us up to see the glory.

The Father's Eternal Purpose

We have in verses 3-5 what is called the doctrine of election. Many people do not like this idea of divine election at all. And their dislike is not without some justification, for there have been real problems with the way this doctrine has been set out in the past. It has been far too exclusive. It has been taken to mean the selection of some and the rejection of others. But here in Ephesians, election is the declaration to us that we are in God's world. It is the proclamation that our world is not an accident, but decidedly purposed.

The great strength of the doctrine of election is that it gives the work of God in creation a very definite purpose. Election, in its supreme sense, means that God creates for a reason. God does not create and then say to Himself, 'Well now, we have this creation, this universe, before us, we have man, what are we going to do with all of this?'

No, it is quite the other way around. God the Father has a purpose first, a clear and definite purpose. And it is in order to bring this purpose to fruition that He creates and calls forth the universe and humanity out of nothing.

On the personal level, this means that you and I are here not by chance, but by design. We are not accidents. We are creatures who have been created by God because He has a plan which includes us.

On the larger level, this means that both the universe, in its staggering immensity and diversity, and human history, in its splendor and complexity, are swallowed up in God's unfolding plan.

Behind everything in creation and history lies the eternal purpose of the Father. That is the secret. And this purpose is no longer hidden from anyone. The reason for all things, including our existence, is no longer an enigma, reserved for the super spiritual or the religious elite. It has been revealed in Christ, the light of the world. The light of human existence, the light of your existence, has been given in Jesus Christ for all to see.

The apostle has seen it. And it is impossible for him to be silent. He is so thrilled he is champing at the proverbial bit to share it with everyone. In fact, he proclaims this secret purpose to us three times in vv. 3-5, and from three different angles so that we cannot miss the point.

In v. 3, Paul refers to this purpose in terms of the Father blessing us with all the treasures of Heaven. That is something of a more concrete translation of the phrase "every spiritual blessing in the heavenly places." Here it is, Paul is saying, the Father's plan is to give us all the treasures of heaven. That is what this creation is all about.

From the very first moment of time and space, all history is worked toward this end. God is good. His plan for us is good, glorious—all the treasures of heaven. And note that it is not the treasures of the earth that God the Father plans to lavish upon us. It is the treasures of *heaven*—and *all* of them.

We are not only in a divine world that, whether we see it or not, marches to the cadence of the divine rhythm. We are in a divinely ordered world that marches toward an absolutely magnificent end. This is what God is about. In eternity, He determined to heap every heavenly treasure upon us.

In v. 4, the apostle refers to this secret purpose as to be made "holy and blameless before Him." In v. 5, he calls this "adoption." Paul is telling us that we are here because God has an eternal purpose for us. And he is declaring to us that God created us so that we would be adopted into His family, included in the circle of His own fellowship, and brought into a life of shared communion.

Adoption! Adoption! Adoption! This is the first thought, the mystery, the secret, of the entire universe. This is *why* this world is here, *why* man, humanity, the universe, history exists. Delete this purpose and there simply is no creation, for there is no reason to call it forth nor to sustain it.

When we stop long enough to ponder, our very existence is quite a remarkable gift to us. We were *not*. We were not here at all. We had no mind, no heart, no eyes to see, no taste buds, no hands to hold, no friendships, no love. We simply were nothing. And we had no power to be.

But God called us forth out of nothingness and not-being and gave us existence. He fashioned us and brought us here. Who cannot but marvel at this? *We* are! We *are!*

But wonderful as it is to *be* and to be *here,* the apostle is declaring to us that the Father has never had any interest in our mere existence. He is telling us that before God created us, He determined that we should be filled and overflowing with His Life—made participants in His life and glory.

You see what is happening here. Paul's mind soars back through time, through the long history of Israel, through the Garden of Eden, through creation and into eternity. And there in eternity, before there was anything, before creation, Paul sees God the Father. And he is allowed to peer into the Father's heart. And there he sees *this* great and glorious purpose for us.

Before there was anything, the Father set out *this* plan and made *this* decision *for us.*

And the cross of Christ, the Father's eternal and beloved Son, reveals that this decision is not a wishy-washy idea or an if-then clause. Nor is it mere political rhetoric. It is decision backed up by divine determination. The Father is excited about His good and glorious plans for us. He is not a wait-and-see God. There are no if-then clauses in His heart. He is zealous. He is filled with unbending earnestness and unswerving determination to see His good plan through to the end at all costs.

Before Him

Let us focus for a moment on this purpose of the Father. We can do this by pondering the phrase "holy and blameless before Him" and particularly the words "before Him."

We have several options here. We could take the expression "before Him" to mean that the Father's purpose for us is to exist, to be created, to appear in His creation and on the scene of His history. While what Paul is telling us certainly includes our existence and appearance in God's creation, he means much more than that here.

The apostle sees a much richer goal in the Father's heart than merely granting us existence—fantastic as that is when we consider the alternative. Paul sees something much more personal. The Father is after a certain *quality* of existence, a certain *form* of human being and life for you and me. It is that we should not only exist, but be in *His presence,* "before Him."

The NIV translates "before Him" as "in His sight." This leaves us with an image of being an *object* in God's sight. Like a chair or a desk or a computer are objects in my sight. But this is far too impersonal, far too pale, weak, and dead for what the apostle has in mind. What he sees is that the Father's eternal purpose for us is not that we should simply *be,* or simply have existence, or merely appear before Him as *objects* in His sight, but that we would be made *participants* in *His* existence, baptized in *His* glory, absolutely immersed in *His* life.

Read carefully this rich statement from one commentator:

BEFORE HIM' denotes the immediate presence of God to man and the closest proximity of man to God. The image suggests the position and relationship enjoyed by the cream of society at a royal court, by children to their father, by a bride to a bridegroom... (Markus Barth, *Ephesians, The Anchor Bible* [New York: Doubleday & Co. Inc., 1974], p. 80).

Do you see this? This is astonishing. Barth says the "*immediate presence* of God to man," "the *closest proximity* of man to God." The point here is not mere existence, but deeply personal relationship, intimacy, fellowship with *God*.

The eternal purpose of the Father is to bring us into existence, and not just into existence but into His house. And not just into His house but to His table, and not just to His table but to His right hand. And not just to His right hand but into conversation with Him, and not just into conversation with Him but into *face-to-face* fellowship with God the Father Himself.

But even here we have not come to the glory of it. For this fellowship is not simply about face-to-face conversation or side-by-side relationship; it is about the meeting and sharing of souls. It is about such a profoundly personal sharing of life, such a thorough exposure of being, that we begin to be *in* God and God begins to be *in* us—mutual indwelling, *perichoresis*.

Paul is talking about being ushered into a fellowship with God that is so close, so intimate, so deep, so real, so alive that everything God the Father is, everything He has, all His treasures and glory are shared with us personally.

Staggering as it may be, inconceivable as it may appear to us, this is what Paul is saying. The Father destined nothing short of *Himself* as our inheritance.

He has no interest in our mere existence. He gives us existence for the sole reason of bringing us into profound intimacy with Him—an intimacy in which God's very being and life and joy pass into us and become ours.

In his book *The Weight of Glory*, C. S. Lewis talks about those moments in our lives when we suddenly recognize beauty. We suddenly behold, we become very aware of, the beauty of something—a sunset, a person, a picture, a word, a touch. We are caught up, for a moment, in the pleasure of what the philosophers and artists of every age call "beauty."

But Lewis goes on to say that, wonderful as these moments are, inspiring and pleasing as they may be, they never really satisfy us. It is not enough to behold beauty. The secret longing of our hearts is to move beyond glimpsing it.

We want something else which can hardly be put into words—to be united with the beauty we see, to pass into it, to receive it into ourselves, to bathe in it, to become part of it. (*The Weight of Glory and Other Addresses* [Grand Rapids: William B. Eerdmans Pub. Co., reprinted 1975], p. 13).

This is a great analogy for what Paul is telling us about God the Father and His eternal purpose for us. It has never crossed the Father's mind to give us mere fleeting glimpses of His glory. The plan from eternity is that we would be included in, united with, baptized into His glory and life.

His eternal purpose for us is nothing less than the gift of passing into, receiving to ourselves, bathing in and becoming part of the Father's very life, security, peace, dignity, joy, purity, freedom and love. Is it any wonder the apostle is so inspired?

Can you believe this? Can you believe that *this* is the way God is, that this is God's will, plan, purpose for *you* from eternity? Can you believe this is why He created you out of nothing? Can you believe that this is why He gives you life now, that this is what your existence, your time, is all about now?

The apostle is bursting at the seams because he has seen it and he knows that this is it. He has heard the conversation between the Father and the Son in the Spirit before creation. He has seen the very heart of the Father. And he is declaring to us that *this* good news, *this* decision, *this* purpose for us was in the Father's heart before the foundation of the world. This is the gospel, the eternal gospel.

Before you were even fashioned in your mother's womb, these cards, as it were, were on the table for you. There has never been any other reason for your existence. God is good. His plans for us are awesome and glorious.

Tailor-Made

Now let us focus on the phrase "holy and blameless." This phrase could be understood legally to mean "not guilty, acquitted in the sight of the Judge." Certainly the idea of being forgiven, without

7

guilt, without *blame,* is present in this phrase. The Father intends that we should be cleansed, without spot or wrinkle. But there is more.

What Paul is telling us here is best understood by concepts such as "fit," "right" and "appropriate." The Father does not want us merely legally clean. He wants us right and ready for Him, formed into fit vessels for His life, custom-made for His presence and fellowship.

One of our first experiences when we tried to set up house in Scotland was the realization that our American plugs did not fit the Scottish sockets. To begin with, there was a different plug design altogether. But that was not the only problem. Our appliances were set up for a different voltage. They were not set up for the Scottish system. We found that our things were foreign, wrong, alien, not right, unfit and inappropriate for the Scottish setup.

Paul is telling us that the Father has planned from the beginning that we would be tailor-made *for Him.* He planned that we would not only come to be, but also that we would be made fit and right *for Himself.*

The plan includes the rejection and overcoming of our wrongness, our foreignness, our alienation. And it includes our transformation into rightness for Him. He not only purposed for us to live, but to be before Him, in His presence. And not only to be before Him, but to be right and fit for Him, tailor-made for fellowship with Him, and sharing in His glory and life.

Adoption

The same point is being made with a slightly different emphasis in v. 5 in the word "adoption." At its most basic level, adoption is a legal concept. It means that one who is not naturally a child is given the place of a natural-born heir, the legal title, rights, and privileges of the family. Even on this level, God's purpose of adoption is quite amazing. The very thought of being given the legal title, rights, and privileges of the family of God is surely stunning for mere creatures.

A legal arrangement, however, is only on the periphery of the apostle's thought. What is meant by adoption bursts the wineskins of

8

mere legal rights and privileges. It is far more personal. Adoption in this context means to be taken into and included in the circle of the Father's fellowship. It means to be included in the circle in which what is shared is not merely rights and privileges, but *life*.

The eternal plan is for the Father to lavish *Himself* upon us, to give Himself and all that He is and has to us, to share with us His own life and joy unspeakable, full of glory. Adoption means to be included in God's very own life, made a participant in His fullness, filled with God.

Moreover, this purpose of inclusion in God the Father's own life carries with it the plan to custom-make us for participation in His life. The purpose to embrace us and include us in His life and fullness incorporates a plan of equipping and forging, tailoring and making us right and ready for Him. For the point is not merely to give us rights and privileges, but to bring us to share in His life.

What good is it for the Father to lavish Himself upon us if we are alien to Him and cannot know Him? Adoption includes the plan of our being made right for God, of our being transformed into at-oneness and union with Him, of our being tailor-made for the Father and His fellowship.

We are here on the brink of a liberating and life-giving vision of Jesus Christ. But before we follow through with this line of thought, we need to pause for a moment and reflect on the amazing point one more time.

Before we were born, before creation was born, before we did anything right or wrong, God the Father determined that we would be brought into union with Him and made full participants in His life and glory. This is the staggering plan in the Father's heart from all eternity. Out of the womb of this glorious purpose creation was birthed and we were given existence. Unto this end we are sustained.

The Chief Executive Officer

Now, grand and glorious as all of this is—almost unbelievable—it is nonetheless, only the beginning of the gospel. In fact, we haven't actually come to the gospel yet. For the apostle not only peered into the Father's heart and beheld this passionate purpose for us. He heard the Father declare to His Son: 'Thou art the One!' 'Thou art the chosen!' 'Thou art the Man of appointment destined to go and accomplish My passion for them!'

You see, volumes are crammed into these little phrases, "in Him" (v. 4), and "through Jesus" (v. 5). Paul is telling us that this great decision of the Father was not made in the abstract. It was made *in Jesus.* We were chosen *in Christ,* predestined to adoption *through Jesus.*

We are coming now to the heart of all things Christian and certainly to the spring of the apostle's inspiration. The very secret of the real Christian life lies right here.

But what do these little prepositions *in* and *through* mean? We must think carefully here, for this is too good to miss. Chosen *in* Christ, predestined *through* Jesus, means that the Father not only planned that we would not be alien to Him but right and ready for Him; He also planned the *way* that He would bring this to pass. And that *way* is Jesus Christ, His eternal Son incarnate. The Father determined *this destiny* for us—embraced, included in the circle of His immediate presence, tailor-made for participation in His life—and He determined the *One* who would accomplish it—Jesus Christ.

This is the gospel circuit blower. For it means that the coming of Jesus is not an afterthought. He was destined to come before the foundation of the world.

Jesus Christ is not Plan B quickly set in motion after the failure of Plan A in Adam. No! No! No! Jesus Christ is Plan A.

He is the only plan. He is the eternal Word (JN 1:1-13, 14). It was all purposed in Him (EPH 1:9). He was always destined to be the One in whom all things would be summed up (v. 10).

From the beginning, the Father planned that His own Son would come and accomplish His eternal purpose for us. Jesus is the Father's eternal CEO. He was charged with the responsibility of making us holy and blameless and bringing us before His Father, before the first particle of creation was called forth.

Chosen in Him, predestined through Jesus Christ, this is the full picture of the gospel.

Adam was never the chosen one. Abraham, Moses, David were never the chosen ones. You were never the chosen one. From all eternity, *Jesus Christ* is the chosen one. He was elected to be the

One who would come and fulfill the Father's plans for us.

We were never designated as the ones who would make ourselves right for the Father. From eternity, that responsibility has been sovereignly snatched from you and me and placed into the hands of Jesus Christ.

Never once has it crossed the mind of the Father that anyone but Jesus would be the mediator, the high priest, the saviour, the executor of His will.

Never once has it entered His mind that you would be responsible for making yourself right for Him. You are not that important in the whole scheme of things. And you are not capable of bearing that kind of responsibility. But Jesus Christ is.

What Paul is telling us is that the Father had His eye on His incarnate Son Jesus Christ when He called creation forth out of nothing. The Father named His own Son before creation and said: 'Thou art the mediator!' 'Thou art the executor!' 'Thou art the vicarious Man!'

Before the beginning, the Father said: 'You, My beloved Son, will go and step into creation.' 'You, My beloved Son, in whom My soul delights, will become a human being, a real man.' 'You will plunge yourself into the midst of human brokenness and eradicate it and forge the real human existence with Me for them.'

'You will invade and attack all alienation and foreignness and replace it with our life and fullness.' 'You will penetrate every fiber of human wrongness and undo it, circumcise and crucify it.'

'You will be their holiness and blamelessness.' 'You will be their at-oneness, exaltation and adoption.'

'You will cross the chasm, all the chasms, between us and bring them to Me—tailor-made, right, and ready for Me and life in My house.'

From all eternity, the Father elected His own Son to be the executor of His plans for us. Here is amazing, and indeed humbling, grace. From the very beginning, the Father put man soundly in his place and gloriously elected Jesus to be the vicarious Man. He planned that *we* would be woven into the fabric of *Jesus'* existence.

From the very beginning, the Father decided that Jesus would be our head and representative and substitute, so much so that what would become of Him would become of us. He planned that Jesus would be the *one* in whom *we* would be radically and decisively cleansed and made right for Himself. He planned that Jesus would be the *one* in whom *our* wrongness would be undone. He planned that Jesus would be the *one* in whom *we* would be taken down and lifted up, emptied and filled with all the treasures of heaven, crucified and exalted into the circle of the Father's fellowship.

From all eternity, the Father planned that *in* Jesus Christ *we* would be crucified, dead, and buried, and made alive again in at-one-ness with the Father.

Chosen *in* Him, predestined *through* Jesus Christ, this is the most exciting news in the universe. This is what has fired the jets of the apostle Paul. He has seen Jesus at the Father's right hand from all eternity and He sees Him there now as a man, as *the* Man, as our head, substitute, representative, mediator and high priest.

The riddle of creation has been cracked wide open before the apostle. He has peered into eternity and seen the Father's great and glorious purpose for us. That in itself has awed him. But he has also heard the Father charge His Son with the responsibility of execution. 'Thou art Saul's, Israel's, the world's Lord and Savior.' And that has thrilled him no end.

It Has Happened

Here indeed is exciting news. But we have not yet come to the full glory of the gospel. For it is not eternity, but *history,* that has set the apostle ablaze. The Word that Paul heard was not merely the Word of the Father spoken in eternity, but the eternal Word of God as it was spoken into historical action. He has encountered the incarnate and risen Son of God. He has seen the Father's Son step out of eternity and into history in the power of the Spirit. And he has seen Him carry out and complete the Father's plans for us. This vision has invaded his being and filled him with hope and joy, inspired him with life, and compelled him to speak.

It is one thing to come to see that there is a God, that this is a divine world created out of divine purpose. It is another to see that this God is fatherly, and that behind it all is the one divine purpose of adoption. It is still another to see that this Father has charged Jesus

Christ, not us, with the work of accomplishing His purpose. But when the seeing becomes breathtaking is when we see that Jesus Christ *has come*.

Paul has seen the Father's beloved Son step into creation in the power of the Spirit. He has seen the Son go to the cross, rise from the dead and ascend to the Father. And He has seen that in *this* act *we* were cleansed, made right and fit for the Father, included and accepted in the circle of His presence and fellowship—even as it was eternally planned.

The Father's purpose has been carried out. It is finished. It has been accomplished in Jesus Christ in the power of the Spirit.

We have been made holy and blameless and brought into the presence of the Father *in Jesus*. We have been adopted and included in the blessed circle *in Jesus*.

This is what has the apostle beside himself with excitement and inspires him with such passion and expectation. And this is why he opens this letter with a gospel *declaration* that doubles as a great shout of praise: Blessed be the God and Father of our Lord Jesus Christ, for He *has blessed us* with all the treasures of heavenly life *in Christ*, just as He planned and predestined before the creation of the world. It has happened. It has taken place. It is now fundamental reality, divine-human reality, your reality.

Stop and drink this in. What Paul is telling us is that the Father's eternal purpose is now accomplished fact. He is telling us that Jesus Christ is the act of the Father by which we were cleansed, embraced and tailor-made for the Father's presence. He is telling us that this is the real truth about us. We have been accepted by God the Father Almighty in Jesus Christ. We have been united with the Father and all that He is and has in Jesus Christ.

Paul is declaring to us that it is not our job to make ourselves right for God. It is not our responsibility to forge for ourselves a foothold in God's existence and fullness. It is not our task to work our way into the blessed circle of God's acceptance.

The Father has charged Jesus Christ with this work and anointed Him with the power of the Holy Spirit, and *Jesus has done it!*

Jesus Christ is the chosen one, the one man of weightiness and significance in the whole scheme of things. He is the secret. His coming and work is the only thing that counts. We are included in Him and His work. Jesus Christ is our humiliation and our exaltation into glory and life.

This is what short-circuited Paul's Pharisaical mind and then became his greatest joy and liberation. The Father designated Jesus Christ to be our saviour, our foothold, our acceptance. And that is who Jesus Christ is, now and forever—our saviour, our foothold, our acceptance. It has happened.

'Thou Art Mine!'

Years ago, my brothers and I would go to the post office with our dad on Saturday mornings. There was this Uncle Sam poster hanging above the door in the post office. It had a caption which said: "Uncle Sam wants you." And in the picture, Uncle Sam is pointing his finger at us.

No matter where you went in the room, Uncle Sam's finger managed to be pointing at you. You simply could not get away from it. We would hug the wall directly beneath the poster and then lean forward just enough to see the poster. No matter, Uncle Sam's finger was still pointing at us. It was inescapable.

That is what the Father is doing now. He is pointing His finger at you and me. He is declaring: 'I have named *you* from the foundation of the world.' 'You are the one, you are the man, you are the woman, you are the child.' 'I created you for life in My house.' 'I brought you forth and sustain you now for the sole purpose of being right for Me and in face-to-face fellowship with Me.'

'And I have destined My own Son to be the executor of My will.'

'And *He* has come and *He* has made you holy and blameless.' 'He has cleansed you of all sin and guilt and wrongness.' 'He has made you right for and with Me.'

'In Him, you have been tailor-made for Me.' 'In Him, you have been exalted into My immediate presence.' 'In Him, I have embraced you and made you Mine.'

This is the staggering and blessed Word of God proclaimed to all creation in Jesus Christ—'Thou art mine!'

Above all things, this Word calls us to be still, cease striving, punch the pause button, and listen. Listen. Listen. Listen. This is the one and only work that we can and must now do. Listening.

'Thou art accepted!' 'Thou art included!' 'Thou art mine!' Hear the divine Word and receive it. Be not unbelieving, but believing. Go over it again and again.

But how hard it is for us to even begin to listen, seriously listen! We are so accustomed to empty rhetoric and hyperbole that we cannot listen. This is too simple. It is too awesome. It is too staggering. It is too finished.

The truth is so foreign to all we naturally assume. It is so foreign to what we think of ourselves and are so sure we *know* to be true about ourselves. It is so foreign to what we have always heard in church! How can we possibly hear the Father's Word?

How quickly we smother the Father's *'Thou art mine,'* sounded in Jesus Christ, with our own "Yes, but..." "Yes, but I am so unworthy." "Yes, but it is quite plain that I am not holy and blameless." "Yes, but in the real world..." As if we are somehow a little more in the know than God. "Bless God's heart, He is such an optimist." "If only God could come out of His ivory tower and trade in the real world for a while." How quickly we give greater weight to what we feel or see with our eyes than to the divine declaration sounded in Jesus Christ.

We get a ray of hope and a bit of liberation and quickly fall back into the bondage of the definitions and expectations and accusations of others. The Father has embraced us and made us His in Jesus Christ. 'Thou art mine!' Who else carries any weight? Why do we listen to the voice of such lightweights? Why do we give their ideas and conceptions and opinions such a place in our lives? God the Father Almighty has spoken and speaks. Listen to Him.

How quickly religious pride rears its ubiquitous head and speaks its own word in us—"Yes, but *you must do...*"—and all that God the Father Almighty is proclaiming to us is instantly discounted. As if we are afraid that this glorious Word of God is powerless; that really hearing this Word and bathing our souls in it will not do anything in us at all, or worse, that it will actually let loose lawlessness and abounding sin.

But this Word is the power of God unto our liberation and life

(ROM 1:16). If only we could hear it. It is the truth which sets us free (JN 8:32). If only we could know the truth.

The Father's 'Thou art mine,' spoken and speaking now in Jesus Christ in the power of the Spirit, translates into food and drink, living water, hope and joy, security and assurance, excitement and passion for fellowship with our Father. It is creative Word, laden with the power to inspire and fill, enliven and set free. 'Thou art mine!' This is the only Word in the universe that carries the power to slay the angst of our souls and produce the glorious liberation of adoption in us. "Yes, *but...*"

The problem lies right here—not in the Word nor in its capacity to kill the dragons that haunt and stifle us so and render us plastic religious androids. The problem for you and me is that we are not quite ready to hear the Word. We still think far too much of ourselves and what we can do and are doing. We still believe in *ourselves*. We still believe that somehow *we can* in fact set ourselves free, or at least that we can do so as well as simply *believing* in the declaration of the Father's lavish embrace.

This hidden faith in ourselves and our opinion of ourselves is the secret source of the smothering "Yes, but I..." All that this "Yes, but I..." means is that we have not yet seen that we are utterly helpless to make ourselves acceptable. All that it means is that we have not yet crashed and burned under the pressure to work our way into the blessed circle of God's acceptance. All that it means is that we have not yet come to see what a mess we are making of ourselves. We have not yet faced the fact that what we are creating in our work for God, in our striving to live the Christian life, is not *life in the Father's embrace* at all, but merely religious nothingness—the mere outward, culturally defined and acceptable form of wholeness and life, service and love. We have not yet seen through our supposed glory and come to the place where we know that whatever else it is, it is vacuous of the glorious liberation of adoption.

For when we come to know that we simply cannot work our way into the blessed circle—when we have been finally baptized in the inescapable knowledge that we do not have this life, are not in actual fact living it, and are in truth powerless to do so, and desperation sets up shop in our soul—*then* we are ready to hear the Word of God. *Then* the simple news of the Father's eternal purpose, carried

16

out and accomplished in Jesus Christ, ceases to be merely religious news and becomes *good* news—inspiring, hope-begetting, joy-producing, liberating and life-giving *Word* to us.

It ceases to be something that we hear and qualify quickly with the "Yes, but I..." and becomes the most blessed thing we have ever heard in our lives, something which immediately sparks hope and assurance and a resounding *hallelujah* within our desperate souls. And there is more life, more genuine Christian reality and humanity, more evangelistic light, in that spark of hope and assurance and in that relieved hallelujah than there is in thirty years of religious doing.

There is more crime-stopping power, more culture-transforming, value-begetting power, in one person who *knows* the truth, who *knows* what God the Father has made *of her* in Jesus Christ, and who thus has assurance running through her veins, than there is in a thousand of our committee-generated kingdoms.

Ours is the day of abstraction. It has been so long since we have heard the simple and pure gospel thundered from our pulpits that our theologians have given over to playing lifeless academic games and our churches have turned to programology to create the kingdom. It is as if we have never seen the Word of God the Father Almighty—sounded in Jesus Christ in the power of the Spirit—do its thing.

Any talk of this Word generating liberation and life appears to us to be pie in the sky optimism.

It is only those who do not yet know they are starving to death who walk away from a feast. The hungry are thrilled at the prospect of food and drink. The hungry eat and drink and are filled, and quite naturally enjoy and share.

Soon we will feel our starvation and will grow desperate. Soon we will come to the end of ourselves and we will be ready to hear the blessed and staggering Word of God sounded and sounding now in Jesus Christ in the power of the Spirit.

God the Father Almighty has embraced you and made you His in Jesus Christ. 'Thou art mine!' Listen! Listen! Listen! This Word is the power of God unto our liberation and life (ROM 1:16).

Amen. Come, Holy Spirit, give us eyes to see and ears to hear. Convert our minds and deliver us from idolatry that we may

Chapter 2 - The Necessity of the Atonement

Ephesians 1:3-8

About 150 years ago in Scotland, a young Church of Scotland minister named John McLeod Campbell began struggling with the question of the atonement, the death of Jesus. He was not alone in this, of course. Every minister worth his salt has struggled and struggles with understanding the whys and wherefores of the death of Christ. But Campbell was one of those men of the Spirit in church history who not only struggled to understand, but whose struggling produced profoundly liberating insights for the church.

His classic book *The Nature of the Atonement* (London: MacMillan & Co., 1856), while somewhat difficult to read, is nevertheless a spiritual gold mine. There are certainly places where Campbell is weak but the book remains one of the most stimulating on the subject to be found.

Campbell was neither an academic theologian nor a professional minister. He was a pastor of the soul. He had no interest whatever in abstract theology or in keeping folk happy. His driving passion was for understanding how to live *life* and with leading his people into the *abounding* life promised to us in the Bible.

Campbell was deeply troubled by the lethargy that he encountered in the spirit of his people. He saw little sign of what Peter calls "joy unspeakable full of glory" (IPET 1:8), or of what Paul calls *"parrhesia"* (assurance, confidence, liberty, boldness).

It was not that his flock was made up of incurably bad people. They were, in fact, good people, and faithful church attendees. But they had little radiance. He found few traces of that simplest yet most healing and enlivening Christian grace, genuine peace.

As one of his parishioners told him on the first day of his ministry, "Give us plain doctrine, Mr. Campbell, for we are a sleeping people." They were not an inspired lot, and while there may have been a steady faithfulness to religious duties, there was little *excitement about God.* Campbell saw that whatever else was happening, Christianity was not producing genuine freedom for God. Instead of kindling a fervent desire to know the Father and inspiring people to draw near to Him, and actually liberating them to enjoy Him and live in His pleasure, Christianity was creating ambiguity and spiritual repression. Instead of assurance, which leads to real relationship with the Father, there was a deep-seated hesitance at work, which led to religious hiding. Something was checking and stifling their spirit.

It was as if a wet blanket had been thrown over the soul of the church.

The relevance of Campbell's wrestling for us today lies right here. For while church means many things to many people, it is doubtful if the description "joy unspeakable, full of glory" is the phrase that most of us would think best describes it. Is it the case that Jesus' image of a river of refreshing water (JN 7:38) fits the contemporary church?

Confidence, liberty, assurance, peace, hope, living in the pleasure of the Father, are these the words that we are forced to use to explain our Christian existence? Do these realities radiate out of the soul of the contemporary church? We do well to follow through Campbell's reflections, for he was faced with the same religious emptiness and impotency we are. And he found answers.

While his book is primarily about the *nature* of the death of Christ, its richness lies in the way Campbell connects the death of Christ with this problem of the spirit. Like every other real pastor of his day and ours, he was burdened with the way the spirit of the age was dominating the soul of his people, and he was dealing with it. The book is alive with his wrestling. He is trying to get to the spiritual cancer. He is trying to understand the wet blanket. He is trying to perceive what has silenced assurance and thus genuine life.

As he wrestles, you can see him tracing the problem initially to the way people thought about God. The people were not sure in their hearts about God's attitude toward them. The people saw ambiguity and hesitance in God toward them. And therefore, instead of overflowing assurance, hope, joy and liberty, which kindle genuine desire to know God, their spirits were stifled, hesitant, lethargic, and fearful.

The Wet Blanket

As a pastor determined to see his people liberated, Campbell set about to address this problem more carefully, to find its root cause and to dig it out. He found that the fundamental cause was that the message of God's staggering love in Christ was not *getting through* to the soul. The Word of the great passion of the Father for us was being obscured. And it was not because the love of God had not been proclaimed.

The people knew all about the love of the Father. But still they were asleep, uninspired, fearful, timid. Something deeper was overriding the message of God's amazing love in Christ—suffocating it. There was *another word* that carried more weight with their soul than the Word of the Father's passion for them in Jesus, which had set the apostle Paul ablaze. There was another message being sounded which short-circuited the liberating light.

Surely some of this short-circuiting of the light resulted from the way the current liberalising of the ideas of father and love emptied the words of their powerful Biblical meaning, such that they increasingly became mere rhetoric. A general notion of the universal fatherhood of God rooted vaguely in God's act of creation, rather than in the act of God in Jesus Christ, does not have the power to disturb a flea, let alone awaken the dead. A grave danger lies here.

But Campbell found that the fundamental problem of the spirit lay in the other direction, namely in the more conservative conception of the atonement. The real culprit was the way the people understood the necessity of Jesus' death. Herein lay the source of his people's spiritual insecurity and lack of energized desire.

He saw that his people understood Jesus' death as being *aimed* at God. Jesus came to satisfy God's justice by suffering the punishment human guilt deserved. Because, they believed, until that justice was satisfied and proper punishment suffered, God could not simply forgive guilty sinners and accept them. Thus, the real reason Jesus came and died was to deal *with God* on their behalf.

It became clear to Campbell that no matter how much preaching there was on the Father's heart, or on the fact that it was the Father who sent the Son, there was another unspoken message heard in the soul: There is a *side of God* that is not for us, that has to

21

be conditioned into being gracious. There is a side of God that has to be dealt with before He can bless us. There is a side of God that has to be satisfied before He can forgive us, before He can embrace us, before He can accept us.

To put this in one phrase, "There is a side of God that does not like me."

It is news of *that side* of God that is the wet blanket. Knowledge of that side of God creates hesitant, uninspired, and self-absorbed Christians. It is this word that generates religion and empty, dehumanizing religious performance. It drains away all yearning to know the Father and stifles all freedom to be near Him, for it creates ambiguity and fear in the soul.

It was news of that side of God that had the attention of the souls of Campbell's people. They heard *this* stifling word every time the *gospel* was preached.

Changing the Goal Posts

So we see Campbell wrestling with the gospel itself and particularly with the presentation and packaging of the gospel that he had inherited. His great contribution lies right here. He changed the goal posts. He took the discussion of the death of Jesus Christ out of the context of law, guilt and punishment, on the one hand, and out of the context of liberal notions of the fatherhood and love of God, on the other, and placed it in the context of the eternal purpose of the Father for us and the threat of its dissolution.

He got first things first. With Paul in Romans 5, Campbell saw that even while we were yet sinners and opposed to God, the Father was nevertheless for us. And with Paul in Ephesians 1, Campbell saw that behind everything lay the Father's eternal purpose of adoption. Campbell put this everlasting goal of adoption at the end of the field and contended that all that we say about Jesus Christ is to be understood in the light of this goal. The secret of the death of Jesus lies here in the purpose of adoption.

The necessity of the death of Jesus Christ does not lie in the satisfaction of *that side* of God that does not like us. Nor does it lie in being merely the supreme *revelation* of a generic love of God for

22

us. It lies in the Father's eternal purpose for us and His relentless faithfulness to it in the teeth of our alienation.

Herein Campbell turned atonement around and viewed the death of Christ not as the act of the Son aimed at *that side of God,* but as the Father's act, the Father's great lightning bolt hurled from heaven, to destroy everything that opposed His one eternal purpose and passion for you and me.

'I want them to be with Me.' 'You My beloved Son, destroy everything that prevents it from being so!'

Here is a God who knows full well about our sin and rebellion and failure, and who maintains His determination that we would be with Him as His beloved. The Father never wavers for a moment over His purpose for our adoption. From all eternity, Jesus Christ has been chosen to eradicate our sin, cleanse us, and bring us home.

Over against the liberal rejection of the penal suffering of Christ at the hands of the Father, and over against the conservative overstatement of Christ suffering punishment from the Father, Campbell perceived the death of Jesus Christ as the consistent act of the Father's eternal passion for us.

Make It So, Number One

There is a great line often repeated in the television series *Star Trek: The Next Generation.* In each episode, there is usually some galactic crisis and Captain John Luc Picard of the Star Ship *Enterprise* calls his commanding officers together to sort things through and form a strategy. After setting out a plan, Captain Picard turns to his number one officer, Commander Will Rikker, and says, "Make it so, Number One."

That is a great line. It is a faint echo of the eternal Word, which precedes all worlds and time and space, spoken by the Father in conversation with His true and faithful Son in the Spirit. 'I want them at-one with Me—make it so, Number One!'

Therein is the necessity of the incarnation and death of the Son of God. It lies precisely in the Father's heart. It lies in His unflinching determination that we should be blessed and included in the Triune life. It lies in His unswerving faithfulness to His purpose.

There was certainly a major obstacle standing in the way of the plans of the Father. But the obstacle was not the Father. The problem was not that there is a side of God that has to be dealt with before He can forgive, embrace, and accept us.

The problem was that you were *there* and He wanted you *here*. You were in the far country and He wanted you home. You were broken, alien and wrong, and He had determined you to be healed, at-one with and right for Him. You were trapped in rebellion, corruption, and death, and He wanted you at His side, included in the circle of His embrace and fellowship, and tailor-made for participation in His life.

The problem was that the Father, *and all His sides,* is relentlessly committed to us. He is determined that we will be with Him. And therefore He shouts an almighty and intolerant *NO!* 'I will not tolerate that form of existence for you.' 'I will not tolerate shallow, fallen, broken existence for you.' 'I will not tolerate your nothingness and death and alienation.' 'You are mine, you belong to Me, in My house, alive in My pleasure.'

'*Therefore,* make it so, Number One!'

'Go into the far country, plunge yourself into their ruin, alienation, brokenness, darkness and estrangement, plunge yourself into the skein of their guilt and corruption, and undo it, unravel it, destroy it and bring them to Me.' 'Crucify that false and broken humanity which is so enslaved to the evil one.' 'Revolutionize their whole being and situation—convert it, transform it utterly.' 'I will be *satisfied* with nothing less.'

That is the necessity of the death of Jesus Christ. The Father made up His mind about us from all eternity. And He will not change. He is uncompromising in His love. Thus, in utter opposition to our alienation, He sends His Son to eliminate it.

A Note on Athanasius

Some 1500 years before Campbell, Athanasius wrote his short treatise *On the Incarnation of the Word* (see *St. Athanasius on the Incarnation,* London: A. R. Mowbray & Co., 1953). He too was answering the question of the necessity of the incarnation and death of Christ. Like Campbell, Athanasius viewed the question against the backdrop of the Father's purpose.

Due to the deception of the evil one and the disobedience of Adam, "the human race," Athanasius writes, "was in process of destruction," "on the road to ruin" (§6), and "wasting out of existence" (§8). "Man…was disappearing, and the work of God was being undone" (§6). In this state of affairs, for Athanasius the question was, "What then was God, being Good, to do?"

> It was unworthy of the goodness of God that the creature made by Him should be brought to nothing through the deceit wrought upon man by the devil; and it was supremely unfitting that the work of God in mankind should disappear, either through their own negligence or through the deceit of evil spirits. As, then, the creatures whom He had created reasonable, like the Word, were in fact perishing, and such noble works were on the road to ruin, what then was God, being Good, to do? Was He to let corruption and death have their way with them? (§6)

The key, for Athanasius, is the goodness of God, which is a statement about the Father's heart. If He was neutral toward us, if He created us begrudgingly, after having His arm twisted in some way, then things would be quite different. But Athanasius knows that the Father's heart was in His creative work. His lavish plans for us did not flow out of lukewarmness but out of determined goodness. Thus the problem: What then was the Father to do when *His purpose* was threatened with dissolution? What then was He to do when *His creation* was wasting into non-existence?

Was He to turn His back and walk away? Was He to be indifferent? Could He be? For Athanasius, the only answer to this question is a resounding 'Of course not!' "It was impossible, therefore, that God should leave man to be carried off by corruption, because it would be unfitting and unworthy of Himself" (§6).

We encounter here in Athanasius the same logic that we find in Campbell. First and foremost, the Father is zealous about His purpose for us. Thus, the deception of the evil one, the plunge of humanity into ruin, and the jeopardizing of our existence were not met with a divine cold shoulder; they were met with quick and stout divine

25

opposition. How could it be otherwise? The Father loves us. Therefore, as the act of the Father's eternal commitment to us and to His purpose for us, the Father sends the Son into battle for us, to wage war against everything that opposes His glorious purpose.

The Expression of the Father's Heart

The gospel is not the news that in dying Jesus dealt with the dark side of God for us. Neither is it the news that in dying Jesus revealed a generic love of God for us. The gospel is the news that there is no dark side of God and that there is no merely generic love of God. It is the news that while *we* were inescapably plunged into dreadful darkness, the Father, in His all-out commitment to us, sent His Son to oppose and remove that darkness at all costs.

The gospel declares to us that, at the Father's command, Jesus plunged Himself into our alienation and ruin. As the fulfillment of the Father's eternal purpose for us, Jesus baptized Himself in our estrangement and took it upon Himself and took it to the cross and destroyed it. And there, as the Father's act, He destroyed our alienation, corruption and false humanity. There, as the living enactment of the Father's forgiveness, He crucified Adam and extinguished the enmity. There, as the self-expression of the Father, Jesus revolutionized our whole being and situation.

At the Father's command, Jesus Christ undid the plunge of Adam, bent back our whole existence and made it right for His Father. That is what happened on the cross. It was our disease, not the Father's; it was our dark side, not the Father's; it was our alienation, brokenness, corruption, and the whole web of our guilt and wrongness that necessitated the cross. For the Father determined us to be with Him and we had become aliens.

It is quite correct to say that the necessity of the atonement arises from the justice of God. But it was not some abstract legal justice which required sufficient punishment before there could be forgiveness. It was the justice of God the Father that arose out of His very being and His one eternal purpose for us. Until that eternal purpose of the Father for us was fulfilled, there was no justice. Until the Father's reason for creating the world, until the Father's plan, was accomplished, fulfilled and enacted, there was not a hint at divine *satisfaction*.

It was the faithfulness, the implacable faithfulness of the Father to His everlasting decision for you and me, that necessitated the crucifixion of His beloved Son. For that was the only way that the plunge of Adam, and our complete ruin in him, could be penetrated to its core and undone. That was the only way our false and alienated humanity could be put to death, re-formed, indeed *recreated,* for Him. The death of the incarnate Son was the only way that the old man and his confusion with the evil one could be sovereignly circumcised and made at-one with the Father.

Jesus Christ is the expression and fulfillment of the Father's eternal love for us. In Him we are brought face to face with what God the Father really thinks of us. Indeed, in His coming and death we are given the revelation of the Father's heart. The whole act of the coming and death of Jesus Christ is the Word of God spoken to us, declaring His unambiguous passion for us. This Word *commands* us to faith and assurance, and to come out of our hiding and know Him and live in His pleasure.

May the Lord grant that this Word would be heard in the depths of our own innermost being, and may He grant that it would drown out every pseudo word and translate into the glorious liberation of adoption.

Chapter 3 - Jesus Christ, God's Answer and Ours

John 2:13-22

The apostle Paul has taken us by the hand and led us to the place where we could see the crack in creation and peer into eternity. With Paul we have seen God the Father's heart and purpose for us before the first particle of creation was called forth. We have seen His passion for us and His plan that we would be with Him as His beloved.

The good news, however, does not stop there. No, the apostle takes us on to see that never for a single moment was the Father's great plan for us entrusted to us to fulfill. It was never intended that we would be in charge.

From eternity, we have been given a mediator. From eternity the Father charged His own Son and named Him the mediator, the messiah, the saviour. From eternity, the Father placed the responsibility of making us holy and blameless and of bringing us before Him, into the hands of His Son, Jesus Christ our Lord.

But again, the gospel does not stop there. For what makes this news so good and glorious is the fact that it has all now been fulfilled. The Son of God has come. The great moment of moments, the event which creation and all history anticipated, has come. The Father's Son, our mediator, our messiah, our saviour, our priest, has stepped into human history and everything has been radically and decisively fulfilled.

This is the good news. This is what the apostle Paul has seen. This is what has inspired and thrilled him. He has seen Jesus Christ with the Father in eternity. He has heard the Father designate Him the CEO of the whole enterprise. And now the apostle has seen the Son of God step out of eternity into time, into our flesh, and carry out His Father's purpose to completion.

All the writers of the NT know that this event is cataclysmic. They feel the shock waves that were sent rippling through the whole universe when the Son of God became flesh. They know the coming of Jesus Christ is the decisive moment in history, in creation, in your existence and mine. They know that here in Jesus Christ everything finds its fulfillment. And the writers of the NT are overwhelmed and driven to think out the staggering implications of the coming of Christ.

This is the secret for all of us. This is the key to the Christian life— knowing what the Father has done with us, with creation, with the world, in Jesus Christ by the power of the Spirit. For it is *this truth* that will set us free, liberate us, and fill us.

There is nothing in all the earth that has the power to liberate us and transform us like the Word of God, the living Word, spoken and speaking in Jesus Christ. And this is the call of the Lord upon us again today—hear the Word, know the truth, encounter Jesus Christ and the passion of the Father in Him.

The way to life is by discovering what it means that the Son of God has stepped into human history, come here, entered into our world and our situation personally. The way to reformation is *via* the apostles, to go back and stand with them and see what they saw, encounter what they encountered, hear what they heard, meet what they met.

This is what the Father would have of this generation and every generation—a fresh knowledge of the meaning of Jesus Christ. It all comes to this. The whole Christian life comes to being still and looking at the Father's Son and seeing what He has done with us in the power of the Spirit. For what He has done with us is astonishing and glorious and alive. The news is so true and good it begins to work in our innermost beings and fill us.

God the Father is not interested in our religion. He is not interested in what we want to do for Him and His glory. He is interested in what He has accomplished in Christ penetrating our souls and beginning to eat its way into our lives. He wants to see what He has already done with us in Christ begin to fill us from the inside out.

That is the road to reformation, renewal, and life. That is the way Christianity works. The news of Jesus Christ begins to live, breathe, and take shape in our desperate souls, and it works its way out into our lives. It is an inside-out reality and it hinges upon the news of God's decisive act in Jesus Christ getting loose in our innermost beings.

The writers of the NT know this. They know that the key lies in the news, the truth, the living Word, getting through to our minds and hearts. The whole NT amounts to a long grappling to communicate with us, to give us eyes to see and ears to hear what God has done with us in Jesus Christ.

This is what John is on about. John begins by saying that Jesus Christ is the eternal Son of God, who was with God and is God, and who has now stepped into human history (1:1-3, 14). And then John proceeds to set before us some very vivid pictures to help us see what this means.

The scene of Jesus cleansing the Temple is such a picture. It is a living parable reported to us with great care by John, and its one purpose is to show us what it means that the Son of God has become human. This is a dramatic picture of the great transformation brought about in Jesus Christ at the Father's command. This is the good news in drama.

Getting our Bearings

The first thing we must do when reading this story about Jesus cleansing the Temple is make sure that we do not miss the absolute drama of this scene. We have to see this incident for what it is.

Note first the contrast with the first part of the chapter. After John announces his theme of the incarnation, he tells us about Jesus transforming the water into wine. This is the first picture, the first *sign,* to use John's word, of the meaning of Jesus Christ. It pictures the transformation and the filling of creation that took place in Jesus' life and death.

This first sign, however, takes place in relative obscurity. It is private and very few people know about it. In contrast, what happens in the second part of the chapter is exceedingly public. It is huge. John tells us that the cleansing of the Temple took place during the Passover celebration. And Passover was one of three annual pilgrimages for the Jews. It was a major event in the national life of Israel, and everything was revolving around the Temple.

Imagine one Easter service for the whole church in the state. Everyone has gathered in one place. It is a veritable beehive. The place is alive with reunions, meals, parties and constant conversation. The gathering is so large we have to tear down the front wall of the largest church building in town so that everyone can see.

In the midst of all the parties and conversations, everyone keeps an eye on the building, the pulpit, the Lord's table, and what is happening inside.

About the time the main service is due to begin, in walks a man. He is young, and the great crowd recognizes Him as Jesus. He walks up to the front and grabs the microphone. We all assume He is about to teach. But instead of teaching, Jesus rips the microphone from the pulpit, jerks the cable from the socket, and starts slinging it around like a whip, running people out of the church. He turns over the communion table and knocks down the pulpit. He shouts at the top of His lungs, "Stop making My Father's house a house of dead ritual, bereft of true zeal and life!" "What is this?" "Where is the real passion for My Father?"

Think of what happened in John 2. This is an absolutely unbelievable scene! This is thunder and lightning! This Man comes in and *cleanses* the *Temple*.

Errol Flynn and Indiana Jones cannot hold a candle to this. This is not special effects. This is real. This is flesh and blood. This is boldness and courage, raw nerve. This is not a limp-wristed, meek and mild, sweet Jesus. This is intense zeal. This is an act of amazing aggression.

Jesus is on the attack here. This is an offensive strike. He has entered into the very heart of human religion, human worship (church on Easter Sunday), and attacked it. He has stepped into the center of Israel's life and cleaned house!

Can you not feel John's hand shaking as he writes this? Can you not see John jumping up and down and shouting, "Look! Look! Here it is!" "This too, just like the transformation of the water into wine, is a *sign* which is telling us what God has accomplished in Jesus."

The point of this story is not to tell us that Jesus was very bold and courageous so that we could be amazed at His boldness and courage. No, the point is to give us a vivid picture that helps us see what Jesus' life and death mean for us.

The whole point of this cleansing of the Temple in John is to

31

teach us about the death of Christ. That is why John makes sure to include the brief dialogue between Jesus and the Jewish leadership (vv. 18-21). They ask for His credentials and authority for such an act. And Jesus enigmatically says something about destroying the temple and raising it up in three days.

The leadership, of course, think He is mad. "It took forty-six years to build this temple, and will You raise it up in three days?" (v. 20). And John adds, "but He was speaking of the temple of His body" (v. 21).

Why does John include this dialogue and make this side comment? Why is this important? He does it so that we cannot possibly miss the point. This scene is about Jesus Christ's life and death and resurrection. John does not want us to think that this incident is merely about Jesus cleansing the Temple. It is a sign of the real cleansing of human existence that takes place in Jesus Himself. It is a graphic picture of what God does to us and with us in the coming of Jesus Christ.

The Divine Invasion

The first thing we must see here is that John is telling us that in Jesus Christ there has been a great divine *invasion*. The Son of God is *here* in human flesh, inside Israel, as a Jew, as a man.

No longer is God over there or up there. Now the Son of God is here.

If we think of the covenant relationship between God and Israel, then the fact that the Son has come here means first and foremost that God has crossed over to Israel's side of the covenant relationship. It is no longer a matter of God on one side and humanity on the other.

Now God is on both sides of the equation. The Father's Son has invaded our turf, the human side of the divine-human relationship. Jesus has entered and stands on this side, our side, your side, of the relationship. This is the general point. God has invaded our human situation.

In the OT we hear God calling Adam and Eve in the garden. "Where are you?" (GEN 3:9). He is calling for His creature, His faithful creature, who answers Him with faithfulness. But that call echoes throughout the whole Bible and throughout the whole history of Israel unanswered. It is never answered. Israel did not answer it. You and I have not answered it. We have all failed and proven hopelessly unfaithful. But here now is the Son of God with us, as one of us, inside our side of the relationship, standing with us under this call. He is standing in the temple.

The eternal plan is here taking shape before our eyes. The Father commanded His own Son to cross the great divide and come to us where we are and invade our situation. He sent forth His own Son, in whom His soul delights, to take up residence in the temple of human flesh. And to do so not just as another human being, but as *the* Man, the *vicarious* Man.

Here, John says, look at this, the Son of God is standing in the temple. He has invaded our situation. He has invaded our place in the relationship and covenant. He has penetrated our responsibility and the place where we are called to answer God.

This is what it means that the Son of God has stepped into history. He stands in your place before God. Your situation, your dilemma, has been invaded by the Son of God Himself. He has taken charge of our existence.

And John is saying, hang on folks, this is not all. Watch what happens now!

The Divine Attack

That the Son of God has come here means not only that our side of the divine-human relationship has been invaded. That is only the first part of the story, only the backdrop for the real drama. What we see here is that the human side of covenant relationship has been *decisively attacked* by God. That is what is so powerfully depicted in this incident.

Jesus is not merely present in the temple. He is not only here with us. He is not only in the bushes with Adam and all of us. He is not neutral. He is not passive. He does not stand there twiddling His thumbs. He does not join in the charade. No! He is on fire for His Father. He is filled with passion for His Father's glory and honor.

He has no toleration for sloth and coldness and indifference. There is no place in His soul for religion. He loves His Father with all of His heart, soul, mind, and being. Thus, in the context of the temple, in the context of heartless ritual, in the context of fallen human existence, He explodes and cleans house. He goes on the offensive. He attacks what is going on in the temple.

This is a window, as it were, into the very existence of Jesus. His whole life is an act of utter opposition to human failure and sloth. This scene in the temple is a vivid picture of the mission of the Son. The Father not only sends His Son to cross over to our side of the relationship, He sends Him to clean house. He sends Him to attack the human failure of the covenant. He sends Him to take up our broken answer and remove it altogether.

The very presence of Jesus and His offensive zeal speak volumes to us. They tells us that God is so *for us* that He does not sit still and wait for us to come to Him. He does not wait for you to be faithful. He does not wait for you to answer His commands. He does not wait for you to get good enough to make it. He does not wait for you to make yourself holy and blameless and work your way to Him. He does not wait for you to offer Him true, sincere and pure obedience.

No, the Father is so committed to us that He sends His Son across the covenant relationship into our situation, our place, our failure. And He sends Him to *attack,* to *clean house,* to replace and reorder the whole situation.

He sends His Son to destroy our failure, our unfaithfulness, our uncleanness, our indifference and rebellion.

He sends Him on an offensive strike designed to undo our wrongness and sin, sweep it all out and turn everything around.

Jesus Christ is on fire for His Father's glory and honor. And He is on fire in the temple. He is on fire inside human existence. He is on fire inside the place where we are called to answer God. And that fire consumes all alienation.

That is the grace of God. That is what the coming of the Son of God means. The Father sends His Son on a mission to seek out and destroy all the barriers that separate us from Himself. He commands Him to enter and lay siege to the source of the enmity and remove it and bring *peace.*

The Father sends His Son to lay hold of our brokenness and

foreignness and take it to the cross and destroy it all. He sends Him to penetrate and utterly remove our alienation. He sends Him to blow the roof off our failure.

That is the mission of the Son of God. 'Go, My Son, enter the domain of darkness, take their place, plunge Yourself into their poverty and bankruptcy and failure, invade the darkness and attack and destroy it all.' That is what Jesus Christ did on the cross of Calvary. He penetrated the core of our wrongness and destroyed it. That is what the cleansing of the Temple is all about. It is a picture of the attacking grace of God in Jesus Christ.

The Divine Filling

But this dramatic scene in the temple is not primarily about cleansing. The attack of Jesus Christ is in truth only a footnote to the larger point. What we see in the temple is *zeal* for the Father's glory and honor. In the first instance, that zeal takes shape in an act of cleansing. But we would be missing the forest for the trees if we stopped here. What is so glorious about this story is that *at last* there is One standing in the temple who is *filling it* with earnest devotion to the Father.

The call of God in creation is here being answered with complete faithfulness. 'Where is My faithful creature?' 'Where is the one I created to be holy and blameless before Me?' 'Where is the one I called forth out of nothing to stand before Me and live in My presence, grace, love and devotion?' This is the question that haunts all creation and echoes within every human soul. 'Where are you, where are you, where are you?' It is the question which irresistibly percolates in the root of your soul—and you have no answer.

But here at last, within creation, within our human flesh and existence and being, One is answering the call.

The Son steps into the stream of human existence where we have all failed to answer the call of God. He steps into Adam's shoes, Israel's shoes, our shoes. And He stands against the whole history of human sloth and indifference, weakness and frailty, obstinance and failure. He shouts an almighty and intolerant No! against it. He attacks and destroys it. He cleans house.

35

But even more than this, Jesus Christ does not leave the house empty. He not only takes away our failure, He replaces it with His own rightness for the Father. He not only removes our false answer, He puts His real answer in its place. He fills the temple with Himself and all that He is before His Father. He puts our name on His answer.

He is our priest in the temple ministering our response and answer to God. He has not only invaded our side of the covenant relationship. He has not only attacked our failure. He has filled our side of the covenant with His own sincerity, integrity, passion and love, holiness and peace and faithfulness.

He answers for us. He is our answer. Jesus is the Father's answer and ours.

The New Call

In His all-out invasion and offensive strike, Jesus has transformed the whole human situation before God. In Him the real exodus has taken place. In Him we have been delivered and brought to the promised land. In His attack, the Son of God acted decisively, once and for all, to deliver humanity from the shackles of sin, alienation and brokenness. And in His offensive assault, the Son acted not only to destroy and deliver, but also to establish a whole new order of human existence.

The answer offered in Jesus Christ constitutes the bursting of the wineskins of the old covenant relationship and the establishment of a new covenant between God and humanity—a new relationship between His Father and us.

At the Father's command, Jesus Christ has forged and made fact a whole new order, a whole new reality of divine-human togetherness. Through incarnation, crucifixion, and resurrection, through faith and faithfulness, He has hammered out a right relationship of peace and fellowship and blessing.

In Himself, in His life and death and resurrection and ascension, Jesus Christ has short-circuited our failure and brought us to His Father.

That is what it means that the Son of God became flesh. Our

estranged, fallen, and broken existence has been invaded and utterly destroyed. Our existence has been refashioned, remade and given new *form* from above. That is the glory of Jesus Christ. He has taken away our alienation and made us holy and blameless. He has crossed the chasm of separation and laid hold of us and brought us, in Himself, to His Father.

In Him, *we are* in a new position, a position of amazing grace, a position of real peace with God, of new relationship with the Father. That is what Jesus has done, accomplished, finished.

We not only stand before the Father's question, 'Where are you?' We stand before His answer in the gospel declaration, 'You are in My Son with Me!' That is the grace of God in Jesus Christ. And herein we find ourselves standing under a new call from God our Father.

The story is told that once while Martin Luther was praying, the devil came and started accusing Luther (for that is what the devil does—he is the accuser of the brethren). The devil started bringing up everything that Luther had done, not done, said and not said, all his faults and failures. As the story goes, Luther turned to him and said, "Is that the best you can do!" "Is that all you know about me?" "Here, let me help you." And Luther proceeded to tell the devil several more of his weaknesses, failures, faults and sins.

But then Luther turned and said, "But that is not all." "Oh yes, I am a sinner, but I am a sinner with an amazing Lord who has taken away my guilt, my shame, my sin, my unfaithfulness and given me a new relationship with His Father."

You see what Luther was doing. He was speaking the gospel truth back to the devil's harassing lie. He was saying in effect, "Don't you dare hound me with condemnation and shame and thus try to make me like a church mouse cowering in the corner, hiding from my Father, when Jesus has brought us together." "Don't you dare try to turn me in upon myself." "I stand in Jesus Christ, cleansed, without spot or wrinkle." "I stand in the Father's staggering embrace in Him." "I am not going back to shame and guilt." "I am not going back to the nothingness of religious performance." "Get out of here!"

This is what the news of the divine invasion, attack and victory of Jesus Christ commands of us. It calls us to believe what God has done and therefore come out of our hiding and live in shameless fellowship with our Father in Jesus Christ. For it declares to us that, at the Father's command, Jesus has brought us to His Father.

It declares to us the astounding news that our relationship with the Father does not depend upon us; it depends upon Jesus. This is the amazing gift of the Triune God to us. We have been given a real relationship with the Father Himself and it does not depend upon us; it is relationship in Jesus Christ—created, forged, and sustained in His faithfulness. We are commanded to bask in it, glory in it, and be filled with it.

The news sounds all around us and demands that we hear it and take it into our souls. It commands us to hear the Word and believe. It commands us therefore to be done with moaning and groaning, to be done with our grandiose and pretentious religious busyness, and to live in the shock of the Father's embrace—with all confidence, assurance and hope.

The victory of Jesus Christ commands us to take in the glorious fact that God the Father has laid hold of us with an eternal grip in Jesus Christ, and therefore to take up the Word and slay the demons of insecurity and fear and hopelessness that so haunt and dominate us. We are called to turn from our endless attempts to justify ourselves and the exhausting burden of proving that we are worthy of being on earth, and to take in the fact that whether or not we ever do one thing that marks our sojourn here as a worthy investment, *He* has justified our existence *in Jesus Christ*.

The news of the victory of Jesus Christ over us demands that we stare the debilitating harassment of loneliness and shame, with their multifarious rippling implications, in the face and boldly proclaim them grotesque illusions—pure lies—dreamt up by the father of lies, for *the Father* has accepted us in the Beloved.

The Word of God effected and sounded in Jesus Christ's invasion, attack and victory commands us to stop trying to answer God, in and of ourselves, and to believe in Jesus Christ, God's answer and ours.

This is what the Father wants—people who understand and believe in His Son and are therefore at *peace*. He wants people who believe that their alienation has been utterly destroyed and that they have been given a real relationship with Him in Jesus. He wants people who see and know and therefore radiate the victory of Jesus' attack from their innermost being.

Not religion, but inspiration. Not people working up a plastic holy life for God, which fools only themselves, but people inspired by the impossible news that *they* have been embraced by God. This is what God wants us to be—a people stunned, with our mouths wide open in amazement, at the news, and thus a people alive with marveling pride in the offensive grace of God in Jesus.

Our Father wants people feeding upon the Word of Jesus, people who dare to believe that *they* have been included, and thus a people boldly going and living where no man has ever gone or lived before— into the very presence of God the Father Almighty and into His joyous pleasure. For that is what our Father planned for us in eternity, and that is what He has now done with us in Jesus Christ in the power of the Spirit.

Rise and shine for your light has come
And the glory of the Lord has risen upon you
Darkness will cover the earth
and the deepest darkness will cover the peoples
But the Lord has risen upon you
and His glory has appeared upon you
And nations will come to your light
and kings to the brightness of your rising (ISA 60:1-3).

Chapter 4 - The Vicarious Man

II Corinthians 5:14-21

If we take away anything from a general reading of the New Testament, we take away the definite impression that the coming of Jesus Christ was a huge event. It generated 27 books by nine different authors. And in one way or another, the theme of every single verse, paragraph and chapter is Jesus Christ and what happened in Him.

All the writers radiate astonishment at what has taken shape in His coming, and they are compelled to help us see it. What Christian does not want to stand where they stood and hear what they heard and feel what they felt? Our aim, in this brief book, is to facilitate just this. It is an attempt to help us touch base with the visceral awe of the early church as it stood in the Spirit before the glory of God in Jesus Christ.

We can summarize what we are seeing in three abstract statements: (1) The Father has a plan for us, a glorious and eternal plan; (2) Jesus Christ has been given charge of this plan and He has accomplished it in history; (3) The Spirit is at work now revealing the victory of Jesus Christ to the world.

These abstractions are helpful in their own way, but they are far from satisfactory. For they are bereft of the relentless passion of the Father for us in His plan, the sovereign glory of Jesus Christ in His victory, and the sheer hope of the Spirit's presence and striving with us and all creation now. It is of paramount importance, therefore, that while we are aiming at conciseness, we nevertheless take the time to move from the abstract to the concrete, so that the truth can touch us and set us free.

We stop the flow for a moment to ponder more carefully the scarlet thread that runs through our whole discussion. It is implicit in all that we have been saying, and explicit at points. But it is so critical it needs to be deliberately isolated and highlighted. It is so fundamental that we need to have it before us again and again.

This "scarlet thread" is what Professor James B. Torrance of

Scotland calls the *vicarious humanity of Christ*.

Every Sunday School child knows that Jesus died for us. He died a substitutionary death. He suffered in our place. But the point of speaking of the vicarious humanity of Christ is to say *He* took *our* place, not only to take away our guilt on the cross, which He certainly did, but to be the substitute of our entire human existence.

This sounds rather frightening at first. But it does not mean that He came to replace us. It means that He came to exchange humanities with us. He came to exchange what *He is* and has with what *we are* and have. He came to take away our alienated humanity and give us real humanity. He came to exchange our broken existence with human existence at-one with and face to face with His Father.

The difference between speaking of the vicarious *death* of Christ and the vicarious *humanity* of Christ is that the one says that Jesus *died* in our place and the other says that *Jesus is* in our place. The one sees His righteousness exchanged for our guilt. The other sees our fallen human existence exchanged with Jesus' human existence with His Father. What is substituted is not merely His righteousness for our sin, but His *entire existence*. His is a vicarious *humanity* in which we are given a new human existence with His Father.

It is the vicarious nature of Christ's existence that lurks as the fundamental assumption behind what the apostle Paul is saying in ROM 5, 2COR 5, EPH 1-2, and COL 1-2. He says, for example, that "the love of Christ controls us, having concluded this, that one died for all, therefore all died" (2COR 5:14). "In Him all the fullness of the Godhead dwells bodily, and in Him you have been made full" (COL 2:9-10).

Perhaps with greater clarity than any other NT writer, Paul sees the decisive *connectedness* between Jesus Christ and humanity. He sees that we are bound up with Jesus Christ. He does not explain it. He does not launch into a long-winded diatribe on how this could possibly be so. He just sees it. Adam has prepared him to see it. One died for all, therefore all died. Through Adam came condemnation and death to all, through Jesus came justification and life to all. In Adam we were emptied, in Jesus we have been filled.

The important point here is that Jesus Christ is not an island.

41

He is not a lone ranger. He is not an American individualist. He is not another disconnected pearl on the endless string of humanity. No! Jesus Christ is the one in whom all the pearls are gathered up, represented, included and dealt with. He is our vicar, our representative and substitute, our minister, priest and mediator, the messiah, the last Adam.

Certainly Jesus was and is an individual. He was and is a single man, a distinct person. But, at the same time, He was and is more than this. He is the "in whom" man—the man *in whom* God deals *with us,* the *vicarious man*.

This is the decisive point for us to see. It is indeed a defining point. Our generation is desperate for definition. We are all on a quest for identity. We are frantic to find our *self,* our *true* self. We turn here and there, in one long and fretful search for ourselves. We move from one thing to another in disheartened dissatisfaction, as we find that the glitter is not gold and the very thing we thought would warm us leaves us cold.

We are empty and we are searching for meaning, real meaning, the kind of meaning that will stick to our ribs like peanut butter instead of dissolving into nothingness like cotton candy. Well, here the search ends. Here we run into the secret. For the apostle is declaring to us that *our self* is bound up with Jesus Christ.

Our identity, who we are, is wrapped up in *that man's* identity. Our true humanity is there in His humanity. Our true existence is there woven into that man's existence. The truth about you and me and, indeed, the world is there in Jesus Christ.

Until we see this, until we see that Jesus Christ is the one in whom we have our existence, our own lives cannot possibly be anything other than a mysterious, angst-producing, enigma to us. Without Him we have no meaning. He is *our* home and there is no other home *for us*.

There are a thousand pretenders, and they all hold out the most grandiose promises to us. But they do not have the goods. For they have no real connection with us. They are not ours. They are all external to our very being and are therefore destined only to frustrate our homesick soul.

But Jesus has *hold* of us. He is not external to our existence; He is the ground of our being, and our *raison d'être* (reason for being). To meet Him and know Him is to find rest and peace for He is simply no foreigner. He is our one and only home. In a quite fundamental sense, to meet Jesus Christ is to meet our *self*.

The Jesus-Gospel Connection

The description of Jesus Christ as the *vicarious man* holds together the two cardinal truths of the gospel. Both have to do with the idea of *connection,* and connection of a rather profound sort. We look now to the first, which has to do with the connection between the message and the person of Jesus. This first connection is the fact that the very substance of the gospel is Jesus Himself and what happened *to Him*.

This truth is quickly being eclipsed in our day. It was at the heart of the theology of the early church. It was recovered in the great Reformation. But it has been obscured again today. We have so focused upon the fact that Jesus died *for us,* it is being forgotten that *He* died. What Jesus did for us is becoming more important than Jesus Himself.

While it is exceedingly obvious that Jesus Christ is the one who suffered and died, somehow the fact that these things happened *to Him* has become less and less significant as we have moved along the way. Somehow the events of His life have become more important than the person to whom they are happening.

The attention has shifted from *Jesus'* death to Jesus' *death.* The focus has become the cross rather than Christ on the cross. And before we realize what is happening, we have flown right past the fact that it was *Jesus* who lived, suffered and rose again and is *now with the Father.*

Without our realizing, Jesus has become merely a means to an end, rather than the end itself. He has become a mere instrument, a divine crescent wrench, as it were, which God picked up and worked with on our broken world—and put back in the toolbox when the work was finished.

We have lost sight of the profound connection between the work of Jesus, and Jesus. They have been separated. And as a result, our most basic conception of the gospel has been deeply marred and confused.

The great work of God in Christ, however, is not merely *through* Christ but *in* Christ. What God does in Jesus, He does *in* and *as* Jesus Christ. It is an incarnational work.

Jesus is not a divine crescent wrench; He is the *incarnate* Son. The great exchange is not about accounting. It is about the Son of God becoming human. The good news is about what has *become of the Son of God*. It is about the change, shall we say, which He is. It is about the change in *His* existence.

The imagery of a crescent wrench implies a clear disconnection between the tool and the object that is being fixed. It is like a mechanic working on a car or a doctor working on a patient. The tool is unaffected. The doctor, at most, gets his hands dirty. But the work of Jesus Christ is not like this at all. It is an incarnational work. He is the doctor who became the patient. He is the mechanic who became the engine. He plunged Himself into our existence and took it upon Himself. He does not work from a distance or from separation. He became flesh. He became what *we are*.

The work of the Son of God lies in the fact *He* became a human being, *He* suffered, *He* died, *He* rose again and *He* ascended and lives now within the circle of the Father's immediate fellowship. He is with the Father now as a human being.

There is the great change. There is the good news. It is the news of *Jesus Christ* and His existence as man with the Father. The fundamental emphasis is not upon what He has done. It is upon who He is and what He has become. The gospel is not about certain isolated events in His life. The gospel is about what has *become of Him* in these events.

This is the first connection that we need to see. The gospel has in view the big picture, the whole *event* of Jesus' existence. It takes in the whole history of Jesus.

We surely pay close attention to the main events of His life— His incarnation, death, resurrection, ascension, for example. But these events are so critical because they are part of the larger *event* of His existence. These events are so important because of what *He* does and is in them, because of what happens to *Him* and becomes of *Him* in them.

We must not lose sight of the forest for the trees. We must keep our eyes steadily upon Jesus *Himself*. That is what the gospel is telling us. Look at this God who becomes flesh and behold what happens to Him, behold what becomes of Him.

What God has done in Jesus Christ is not like a robe which has nothing *per se* to do with Jesus Himself. A robe can be taken off and put in the closet. The door can be closed and the robe is done with. It is merely clothing. It is extrinsic. It has no connection with the person. But what God has done in Jesus cannot be taken off Jesus. It cannot be removed from Him. It cannot be placed somewhere else. It is too much a part of who Jesus is. It cannot be disconnected from Jesus at all, for His very existence as a human being with the Father is the work of God.

The good news is not about what the Son of God did; it is about what the Son of God is and has in and through what He did. The gospel has in view the whole seamless event of His personal existence, from the womb of the virgin Mary to His human session at His Father's right hand in glory. It is the good news of Jesus Christ, of His human existence and what became of it.

The Son of God became human. And He took His humanity through death into resurrection and into the embrace of the Father. He became flesh and *as man* He died, *as man* He rose again, and *as man* He ascended to the Father. Here we come to the essence of what it means that the gospel is the good news of *Jesus Christ*. The Son of God became a human being and hammered out a human existence with His Father in the Spirit. He became human and did away with the false humanity and forged a new human existence. He is the new human existence.

He is no mere instrument which is used for a higher goal. No! He is the goal. His human existence with the Father is the prize. He is Himself the reality of the change.

Now, *as a human being,* as man, He is face to face with His Father. Now, as man, He dwells in the Father in utter at-oneness. Now, as man, He lives in the circle of His fellowship in the Spirit. That is the gospel; it is the good news of *Jesus Christ,* of His existence as a human being with the Father in the Spirit right now.

This is the point for us to recover. The Son of God became son of man and now lives as man with His Father in the Spirit. He became a human being and has taken His humanity to the Father. This is the change of changes. It is all about what has become of the Son of God.

The Jesus-Us Connection

As we noted, the description of Jesus Christ as the substitutionary man, the *vicarious* man, brings to expression the two cardinal concepts of the gospel. We have been focusing upon the first, namely, the decisive connection between Jesus Himself and the news. The gospel is not the news of what God has done *through* Jesus, but of what God has done *in* and *as* Jesus Christ. It is the good news of the Son of God's human existence which He has forged in utter at-oneness with the Father in the Spirit. Now, we turn to the second cardinal concept, which also has to do with the idea of connection. But here the connection is not between Jesus and the gospel, but between Jesus and us.

We have been pounding home the point that the gospel is the good news of *Jesus Christ*. But now we think about the fact that the gospel is the *good news* of Jesus Christ. In other words, we turn our attention now upon the fact that what has *become of Him* is good news *to us*.

In the first instance, the gospel is strictly concerned with the Son Himself and what became of Him. In the second instance, the gospel is concerned with the fact that this was a vicarious act. *We* were and are implicated in Him and what became of Him.

It is one thing to see the Son of God *as man* now with His Father. It is another to see that you and I and the world are bound up with Him. Here we are standing before the awesome fact of Jesus as the vicarious man. It is this fact that makes the gospel truly *good* news to us.

The apostle Paul sees that Jesus Christ is no lightweight in the whole scheme of things. He sees that while Jesus is an individual and while He alone died and rose again, nevertheless, this was the act of God dealing with all of us. In his own words, "God was in Christ reconciling *the world* to Himself" (2COR 5:19). He reconciled *us* in Christ (v. 18).

We need to think carefully about this, for life rides on it. It is one thing to say that God has done something in Jesus which can be our reconciliation. It is quite another to say that God *reconciled us* in Christ.

The one leaves us outside of the events of Jesus' life. The

other implicates us in Him and what happened to Him. The one says God did something *for us* in Jesus. The other says that God did something *with us* in Jesus.

The one presupposes a disconnection between Jesus and us. He is over there, we are here. The other assumes a decisive connection. He is there and I am bound up with Him. I am implicated in what became of Him.

The apostle is telling us that God was not only in Christ acting, but that He was reconciling *you* and *me* in this act. In Jesus, God was doing something *to me, to you, to the world.*

The old hymn poses the question, "Were you there when they crucified the Lord?" and St. Paul is answering with a resounding "Yes!" He sees that this one act has cosmic significance. He sees our identification, our connection, with Jesus Christ—or rather, His identification and connection with us. He sees Jesus' Headship and Lordship over us. He sees that you and I were bound up with Christ and what happened to Him. He sees that God dealt *with us* in Jesus. We were decidedly implicated in this one act of God.

The apostle Paul has seen Jesus Christ named in eternity as the one destined to fulfill the Father's passion for you and me and the creation. He has seen Him elected to be the mediator, the CEO, as we have called it, from before the foundation of the world. And He has seen the Son of God step into history. And he sees that what goes on here *in* Jesus, in His existence, is not of some peripheral, perhaps-some-day, significance for you and me. No! Paul sees that the incarnation of the Son of God is an event of scandalous divine sovereignty in which God—quite apart from our permission or vote—threw a lasso around us, gathered us together, and dealt with us.

The incarnation is an act of profound identification and connection with us. How can we grasp this? We are Americans. We are independent. We are rugged individualists. We are taught from our mother's womb that we stand on our own feet. It is crammed into our little brains from day one that we are our own men and women. And every day the whole system preaches to us that our identity is found strictly in ourselves.

The apostle Paul, however, is here taking a sledgehammer to this deceived and darkened notion. He is declaring to us that this is a lie. It has never been true. We are not individuals at all. There is no "just me," standing on my own. He is declaring to us that we are bound up with Jesus Christ. We are connected to Jesus. He is our Head and Lord. He is our mediator and priest, our representative and substitute. His coming means that we do not stand alone; we stand in Him.

Humanity, with all its independent individuals, has been encircled and gathered up in God's humanity. Humanity has been narrowed down to and focused in Jesus. He has summed up all things in Himself (EPH 1:10).

Is the incarnation of the Son of God less profound than the creation of Adam? Why should we give Adam greater weight in the creation than Jesus Christ? He is the *Son of God*. It is the *Creator,* not another creature, who became human. At the very least, His connectedness with the human race is as solid as Adam's. Should it not be that if we err here, we err on the side of the great surpassing superiority of Jesus Christ over Adam? Should it not be that instead of an ambiguous "Yes, but..." there should be a rather resounding "how much more so?"

As surely as we were all caught up in Adam, we have been caught up in Jesus Christ, and even more so. For when the Son of God stepped personally into the equation of human existence, Adam the creature ran up against God the Creator and was rendered a cosmic lightweight.

If all Israel was implicated in the act of the high priest when he went into the holy of holies, how much more implication we ought to see when the *Son of God* became human and entered into the real Presence!

How can we interpret such a radical *divine event* as the incarnation of the Son of God as anything but an astounding act of substitutionary identification with us? He is the One through whom all things were made and in whom all things exist. Delete Him and all creation evaporates.

When *He* steps personally into the equation of human existence, it is not a peripheral moment for you and me. It is not back page, small print, news. It is a decisive act of sovereign Lordship over us. It is the act of God whereby we are gathered up. This is the *Son of God*.

For good or ill, when *He* steps into human existence, what

becomes of Him becomes *of us*. For good or ill, what happens to Him, happens *to us*.

This is what has gotten hold of Paul. He has seen this identification, this divine-human connection in Jesus, this Jesus-us connection. It is huge. It is sovereign. It is decisive. Jesus Christ is not merely a man—He is *the man,* the *vicarious* man, in whom we are decisively implicated.

The Promise of the Vicarious Man

The Son of God became a human being and through fire and trial, through crucifixion and resurrection, forged a human existence in utter at-oneness with His Father. Now, as a human being, He dwells in the very glory and life of God. Now, as a human being, He lives face to face with His Father, secure and fully sharing in all that the Father is and has in the Spirit.

Jesus Christ, however, is *with* the Father now not only as a man, but as *the* man, the *in whom* man, the *vicarious* man. And that means that His very existence as man with the Father, His very humanity at-one with God, constitutes *our* reconciliation and glorification.

Jesus Christ, crucified, but now alive and with His Father, is the justification of *our* existence. He is the act of our inclusion and adoption.

The gospel confronts us with the amazing news that in Jesus Christ *we* have been cleansed, reconciled and glorified. In Him *we* have been taken into the very life and glory of God.

On the one hand, this reality is never to be separated from Jesus Christ. *He alone* is the justified and glorified man. He alone dwells in the Father. On the other hand, He is never to be separated from us. *We are* included in His justified and glorified existence.

This is why the early church proclaimed Jesus not only as our saviour but as our salvation itself. For they saw these two great connections in the gospel. They believed in the incarnation. They believed in the continuing reality of the Son's humanity now and for eternity. They saw the Son of God become human and go, as man, to the Father. And they saw the glorious, yet scandalous, connection that He has with all of us. This was a vicarious act. His very existence with the Father as the incarnate, crucified yet resurrected and ascended, Son *is* the atonement between God and humanity.

He is, at-one, utterly and completely at-one, with the Father in the Spirit. And He is at-one with the Father *as* the vicarious man.

His existence is the very reality of *our* at-onement with God. It is our reconciliation. He is our justification. He is our peace with God. He is our glorification and adoption.

We have not yet heard the gospel until we hear this. We have not yet seen the glory of Jesus Christ until we see His existence with the Father as the glorious truth about *our existence.* For in and as Jesus Christ, God laid hold of you and me and the world, did away with our false existence, and recreated us in union with Himself. That is what the vicarious humanity of the Son of God means: *He* is *our* union with God.

Now, it is the very *reality* of our inclusion in Jesus and His life with God, it is the very fact that *He,* as the vicarious man, is *our* home with God and the universe, that creates the promises—and the warnings—of the gospel. Or, to put this another way, it is the fact that Jesus Christ is now our reconciliation that creates the basis and necessity of faith. It is the fact that Jesus Christ is the One in whom our existence is justified and glorified that makes the Word of Jesus Christ so existentially powerful.

Apart from Jesus Christ, there is no justification for your presence in creation. You have no other ground for being at all. Were it not for the fact that He is *with* the Father, were it not for the fact that *He,* as man, as the vicarious man who has connected Himself with you, is *in God,* you would not be. You have no other foothold in God's existence. His place with the Father, as *the man,* is your acceptance, and thus your only hope and security. Without Him you have no surety, no anchor in life. Without Him you have no guarantee for continuing to be.

It is the grace of God in Jesus Christ, it is the very faith and faithfulness of Jesus Christ, the vicarious man, that holds you and me out of nothingness and gives us existence. For He is the only union God has forged with us. There is no other connection with the existence and life of God at all.

From a negative vantage point, this means for you and me

and every person in the world that ignorance of Jesus Christ, ignorance of what God has made of us in Him, is no peripheral matter. Ignorance of Jesus Christ can lead only to despair of the profoundest kind. For it is only the knowledge of Jesus Christ, and what we have become in Him, that has the reality and power to convince us that our very existence is not in jeopardy.

It may be that the sheer jeopardy of our existence has never crossed our conscious minds. But that is not to say that we do not know it. Far from it. The deepest and most powerful knowing in our lives is the knowing of the soul, the knowing of the innermost man. And it is there, at the inner recesses of our being, that *we know* that our very existence is threatened. How could it be otherwise? Only in Christ is our existence secured.

The one who does not know what God has made of him in Christ is not sitting there with a peaceful soul, calm, confident, and secure. On what basis could there possibly be any real calmness or genuine security? It is impossible.

Our only security in the universe is the fact that Jesus Christ is with the Father and that we are included in Him. Ignorance of this fact does not leave our souls at ease in some comfortable neutrality; it leaves them profoundly dis-eased. Frantic! Racked with insecurity. Scared to death. Overwhelmed. Hopeless.

Read carefully the following epitaph that I once found etched on a grave stone:

> The march of time will see
> that you are here with me
> and you too will be forgotten

This is what the soul ignorant of Jesus Christ knows—the inescapable haunt of impending nothingness. And the soul knows that it has absolutely no way of shouting the haunt down and silencing it. Only the Word of God sounded in Jesus Christ has that kind of reality and power. For only in Jesus Christ has the threat of nothingness actually been overcome.

Only in Him have we become something. Only in Him do we in fact have a foothold in eternal being. To be ignorant of Him means the slightest whisper of nothingness throws the chains of angst around our souls. For we have no answer in ourselves and there is no other answer. We have no way of silencing the menacing whisper—'Thou wilt cease to be!'

If we do not know ourselves to be participants in Jesus Christ, included in His justified existence and at-homeness with God, we are far from a comfortable neutrality. We are nervous wrecks, incurably laboring under the harassment of guilt and shame and the threat of our disintegration.

Without knowing Jesus Christ, what hope is there of ever experiencing peace, personal unity, or wholeness? How could there be any congruence between our insides and our outsides? How could there be any harmony between our soul and our humanity? How could we have any real freedom to be? How could we have any authentic enjoyment of our existence? Jesus Christ is the only reason that our existence does not evaporate.

Only the knowledge of Jesus Christ, and of what the Father has made of us in Him, has the reality and power to produce peace, assurance, hope and joy and freedom in us. Delete the knowledge of Christ, and our lives, our relationships, our work and play, our going and coming, all become variations on the theme of spiritual angst.

The haunt of nothingness drives us to prove ourselves, to demonstrate that we are people of consequence. We become enslaved to everything that holds out any promise—career, prestige, money, athletic prowess, power, religion. We prostrate ourselves to be accepted. We play the game, any game, so long as it holds out some semblance of reality.

We create empires of imaginary glory in the hope that somehow they can make us something. We become wizards of rhetoric in the faith that a plethora of hype will actually create something real.

We become aggressive and impatient and angry, or depressed and withdrawn. We become gossips and slanderers, for tearing down others gives a moment's solace to our own fear of nothingness. We become workaholics, busyaholics, religaholics, couch potatoes and drunkards, for we cannot bear to feel the haunt.

Without spiritual knowledge of Jesus Christ, and what our Father has done with us in Him, we become utterly self-centered and incapable of real friendship and love. For our soul is desperate to protect itself. Whatever relationships we have, we have only for our own benefit. For there is no possibility of freedom to give up ourselves for others when there is no assurance that we are eternally secure.

Without spiritual knowledge of Jesus Christ, we are not neutral people. We are dominated people. We are harassed and already pitiful. For we have heard no Word from the only One who counts and can speak with actual authority. We therefore have no genuine rest, no peace, no hope, no meaning, no security. Without the Divine Word of assurance we inevitably become psychological, physiological, and relational expressions of angst. It irresistibly forms itself in our human being. This is what ignorance of Jesus Christ, and of what God the Father has made of us in Him, creates in us—hell!

But spiritual knowledge of Jesus Christ is the beginning of the end of all of this for us. To know Him is to see ourselves in a new light, a light which begins to cure the soul and set it free for life in the Father's pleasure. For the light of Jesus Christ dispels the terrible darkness that so haunts the soul.

The gospel promises joy and peace, hope, assurance and fullness and abundant life to us. It promises us security, dignity and glory and freedom to love. In place of a withering soul, the gospel promises that a river of living water will well up within our innermost beings and flow to others.

The gospel does not promise these things to us because it is confident in us, or in our ability to be good Christians or apply religious principles to our lives. God forbid! It promises these things to us because it knows about our angst and it knows that Jesus Christ really is our salvation. It knows that God the Father has indeed embraced us in Him.

Thus, it knows that to encounter Jesus is not to encounter merely another good idea, or another clever bit of philosophy, or another promising self-help program—all of which are only as good as we can manage to make them. No! The gospel knows that to encounter Jesus Christ is an event which strikes to the root of our being. It knows that to encounter Jesus Christ is to encounter a living truth, *reality*, which does not sit idle but goes to work in us.

Jesus Christ does not come to us as an abstraction. He comes to us clothed with His gospel, as the light of *our* life, the truth about *us*. To hear the news of Jesus Christ is to encounter the fact that our existence is not threatened but secured by God, that we are not guilty but justified, that we are not lost but found, that we are not alone but included. It is to hear a Divine Word that speaks peace, joy and hope and security into the innermost recesses of our being. It is to hear a Word that invades the stronghold of our angst and dread and begins to slay them.

If Jesus Christ were a mere theory or hypothesis, then His news would have no real promise for us. It would not have the power to affect us. It would come to us only as a dead word, rather than the living, active, and creative Word of God which has the power to quicken hope and assurance within us. For it would be only another bit of religious information which is external to us and has no actual bearing on our being and existence. It would not come to us as truth, our truth, the truth about us.

The gospel, however, declares to us that Jesus Christ is our Lord, the sovereign victor over us and our existence. It proclaims to us that *we* are participants in *His* justified existence, that *we* are participants in *His* glory and life with the Father, that *we* are in *Him* who has overcome, and is secure and alive. It proclaims to us that in Him God the Father Almighty has laid hold of us, snatched us from nothingness, embraced us and brought us home. It negates the epitaph and its oppression.

The gospel of Jesus Christ does not come to us as theoretical or abstract information which has no reality in it; it comes as living truth. It comes to us as loaded truth, laden with the reality of our peace with God, laden with the reality of our security, laden with the reality of our justification and glorification in Him.

To see Him, to behold His place and glory in the whole scheme of things, to see the great and awesome thing that God has done *with us* in Him, is to hear the Father declare 'Thou art mine!' And to receive this Word is to have it reverberate a resounding *Yes!* through the core of our being. A *Yes!* which blows the gates of our shame and fearful hiding off their hinges. A *Yes!* which baptizes, bathes, immerses our souls in the confidence of the Father's acceptance.

To see Jesus Christ with His Father in the Spirit, and to see Him there not only as man, but as the vicarious man, as *my man,* is the beginning of *life.* For it is to see ourselves in Him embraced by the Father Himself, and it is thus to come under the spiritual influence of seeing our actual security and peace and hope in Christ.

Seeing ourselves bound up in Jesus Christ is the beginning of freedom from our profound self-centeredness, which wreaks such havoc in our relationships. It is the beginning of freedom from the menace of nothingness which goads us to create and become enslaved to all our systems. It is the beginning of the end of empty religious performance in all of its forms, for it is the beginning of actual freedom for relationship with God the Father Almighty and living life in His pleasure, and sharing that life with others.

For to see Jesus Christ as the vicarious man is, at last, to see the shocking truth about ourselves—cleansed and accepted, justified and embraced. It is to see ourselves not alone, but included; not guilty, but forgiven; not alienated, but reconciled; not adrift in the universe, but found in Jesus Christ and at home in the Father's good pleasure. And that sight is indeed glorious and powerful, quickening and liberating.

Amen and hallelujah. Come Holy Spirit, shine the light of Jesus upon us.

Chapter 5 - The Education of the Human Race

I Corinthians 2:12, John 16:5-15

In our last chapter we talked about the two cardinal connections of the gospel. The first is the connection between Jesus Himself and the message. The gospel is the good news of *Jesus Christ*. It is not the news of what He *did*, so much as it is the news of what the Son of God *became* and what *became of Him*. The Son of God became human, and now, as a human being, dwells face to face with His Father. For all eternity, He will be human. For all eternity, He will share fully and completely, as a human being, in His Father's being and life in the Spirit.

In the first instance, the gospel is the news of what has happened to the Son of God. He has become human, and through living, through crucifixion, resurrection and ascension, He—as man—dwells now and forever inside the circle of the Triune life and glory of God.

The second connection is between Jesus and us. In sovereign grace, the Father implicated *us* and bound *us* up with Jesus and what became of Him. Jesus Christ is not merely another individual man—He is the Son of God as man. He is *the Man,* the One in whom the Father laid hold of you and me, cleansed us, accepted us, and made us participants in the very life of the Triune God.

Jesus is the *vicarious man.* In what became of Him in incarnation, death, resurrection and ascension, *we* have been recreated and ushered into the Father's immediate fellowship and super-abounding *life*.

In the second instance, the gospel is the good news of the decisive connection between Jesus Christ and us. It is the news of our inclusion in Him and in His justified, reconciled, and filled human existence with His Father.

Therein lies the heart of the gospel. It is the news of what became of *the Son of God* and of what became of *us* in Him. It is the declaration to us that we are not alone, but divinely bound up with Jesus with His Father— in Paul's great phrase, "You have died and your life is hidden with Christ in God" (COL 3:3).

The Glaring Discrepancy

It does not take a brain surgeon to discern, however, that what has become of us in Jesus, the vicarious man, is a far cry from what we experience in our lives now. There is a glaring discrepancy between what the Father has *made of us in Jesus* and what *we are in ourselves*. In Jesus, we are justified and reconciled, at-one with the Father, alive in His life and glory. In ourselves now, we are far from experiencing this justification, reconciliation, and life. Our lives are more a form of hiding from God and one another than they are a form of at-oneness.

Why is this? Why this glaring discrepancy? If the Father has embraced me, reconciled me, justified me, and adopted me in Jesus, why then is my life the way it is? Where is this embrace and reconciliation? Where is this glory and at-oneness?

If God has reconciled the world in Jesus, why is the world such a mess? If He has established *shalom* in Jesus, then why are our relationships so broken and shallow and the earth riddled with such violence?

If God has recreated creation in the vicarious man, and given us not merely a fresh start or a new legal standing, but a new humanity at-one with Himself in Jesus, why then the conflict, why the greed and selfishness and the "bent to sinning," as the hymn writer put it? Why the empty religion? Why the depression, anger, and cynicism? Why the frustration and struggling? Why the hatred and bitterness and enmity? Why the suffering? Why the chaos? Why do we feel so empty and lost?

If the Father has exalted us into the very circle of the Triune life of God in Jesus Christ, why then is there so little experience of this—even in the church?

What has caused this fantastic breach between "who we are in Christ" and "what we experience in our lives now"? What is responsible for this big ugly ditch between "what God has made of us in Jesus" on the one side, and "what we feel and see, taste and know now," on the other? What has caused and continues to create such an appalling distinction? What keeps us from experiencing to the full the life and relationship with the Father and with one another, and with creation, that is ours in Jesus Christ? What stands in the way? What is it that hinders us from being our true selves in Christ?

It is not Jesus Christ who produces brokenness and shallowness and fearful hiding. It is not Jesus who produces anger and depression, weariness, or lust and greed. It is not Jesus who produces hopelessness, or impetuous busyness, or prostrating enslavement to the system. Jesus Christ does not produce chaos or self-centeredness. He produces life.

The question that must be answered is this: What is it that produces these things in us? What is it that creates this form of human existence? What is the secret power at work here which wields such force in our lives? How does it operate and get control?

And a better question still is: What is God doing about this harassing and dominating power? Has the Triune God left us to ourselves now? Has the Father reconciled us and exalted us into the circle of His immediate fellowship and blessing in Christ, only now to leave it to us to figure out how to live in this glory? Has our Father gone to such lengths to plan our salvation and execute it in Christ, only now to turn His back upon us and let us find our own way? God forbid! The Father, in the name of the vicarious man, showers the Helper, the Holy Spirit, upon us.

"And He, when He comes, will convict the world concerning sin, and righteousness, and judgment." And "the Spirit of truth...will guide you into all the truth" (JN14:8, 13). "Now we have received, not the spirit of the world, but the Spirit who is from God, that we might know the things freely given to us by God" (1COR 2:12).

Spiritual Mechanics

The phrase *spiritual mechanics* is somewhat of an oxymoron. We do not normally associate mechanics with spiritual matters. But the truth is that our outward acting and being are bound up with an inner mechanism which is spiritual. We do what we do because of what is going on inside us. Our outward actions are the fruit of inward dynamics. Our relationships, or the lack of them, are shaped by what is happening within us. We live, we act and react, respond and relate, from the inside out.

We have all thrown a rock into a pond and seen the way it

creates a series of ripples, concentric circles. Each of those circles is, in essence, an extension or expression of the inner circle. That is the point for us to see here. Our values and interests, our feelings and emotions, our outlook and interpretations, our acting and reacting, our relating and responding are all extensions or expressions of the inner circle of our being. We live from the inside out.

It is all very spontaneous and involuntary, which is to say that we don't have to think about it and then do it. It simply happens. What goes on inside of us inevitably expresses itself in outward action and reaction—it takes human form.

The story is told about a pastor who forgot to dismiss the younger children after the children's sermon. He realized what he had done as two of his own children got a good case of the heebie-jeebies and began squirming all over the pew. For all young children, sitting still in church—or anywhere, for that matter—is merely an abstract concept. When it came time for the pastoral prayer, the preacher announced the prayer and the congregation bowed. In that split second between bowing and praying, the preacher made eye contact with his children, who were vibrating on the second row, and mouthed the words "straighten up" to them.

A feeling of horror rushed through him as he noticed that a lady sitting on the front row sat up abruptly and looked at him with shock and disbelief. She was sitting directly between the pastor and his children and thought that the pastor was addressing her.

Who knows what went through her mind as she perceived the preacher to be telling her to "straighten up," in front of the whole congregation! Later, the pastor said that he did not know the lady and saw only a blur as she darted out the front door without speaking!

Humorous as the story is, unless, of course, you are the lady, it gives us a concrete picture of how our insides shape our outsides. What goes on inside us quickly expresses itself in action and reaction. It wasn't that the lady had to think about all of this logically. She did not have to reach the conclusion that she should be embarrassed and angry at the pastor, and that she should therefore go and apply that embarrassment and anger in her relationship with him. It just happened. What she perceived shut down her capacity for relationship—it took relational form.

It was spontaneous. It dominated her whole attitude toward

the service and the people around her. Her inner circle rippled into response; it expressed itself in her relating or non-relating.

Let me give another illustration. Two children are playing in the den with their father and mother. They are having a ball, laughing and being silly. It is a scene of complete freedom, at-homeness and joy. A friend of the father's rings the doorbell. He is invited in and sits down on the couch. The children stop playing and grow silent. The little boy pulls his baseball cap down over his eyes. The children cling to their mother and father. They move to the corner of the room and crawl under a table and begin to play quietly.

The whole scene has dramatically changed. One moment there is freedom to be, the next there is stifled hiding. One moment there is exuberant joy, the next there is insecurity and silence. It is not that the children had to think about this. They perceived the father's friend as an intruder, an alien, perhaps even a threat or an enemy. And their inner perception took immediate shape in their outward being and acting. Their perception applied itself to their demeanor; it rippled into their relationships. Their insides expressed themselves in their outsides.

Now, these stories are simple and, more or less, surface illustrations, but they help us to see that there is such a thing as spiritual mechanics at work in our lives. They help us to see that we are spontaneous creatures; we live spontaneously from the inside out. Moreover, they help us see that this "inside," which exerts such influence upon us, is perception, knowing, believing.

One of the great Bible words that gathers all of this together, and gives it a much richer and deeper twist, is the word *soul*. The soul is the center of our humanity. It is the inner circle, the core, the innermost man. It is not like a finger or a leg—not one part which fits together with other parts to make up our humanness. The soul is the point at which everything about us integrates. It is the hub of our physical, intellectual, emotional and relational humanity.

The soul is like a fountain which flows into every dimension of our existence. What happens in the soul spontaneously expresses itself and takes form in life. In other words, the reason we do what we do, act the way we act, and react the way we react is because of what goes on in our souls. In a quite simple yet profound way, *we are* the expressions of our souls.

We love to talk about freedom in America, but there is no freedom whatsoever here. None of us is free from our soul. Its physical and emotional and relational influence is inescapable. The soul *applies itself* to us. That is just the way we are designed.

Think about an onion. There are layers and layers. But in essence, every layer is merely the expression of the inner core. This inner core for us is the soul. And it has a mind of its own, as it were. It sees. It hears. It believes. It knows. And what it sees and hears, knows and believes, spontaneously takes form in our attitudes and feelings, and expresses itself in our relating and responding to everything around us.

What goes on in our innermost being does not have a mere peripheral bearing upon us. It is the hidden secret of our living. It is, in the most fundamental sense, *why* we are what we are, *why* we act the way we act and do the things that we do.

The Real Problem

The glaring discrepancy between "what God has made of us in Christ" and "what we experience in our lives now" has its human cause right here in the soul, and specifically in what our souls know and believe.

While I do not want to be overly simplistic, the plain truth is that it is the *knowing* of the soul that produces our angst and dis-ease. It is the *perception* of the soul that produces our lust and greed, our frustration, anger and depression, our impetuous busyness and enslavement to the most readily available system of somebodiness. It is the *believing* of the soul that produces the hiding and brokenness and pitiful shallowness in our relationships.

There are, of course, many other factors that have to be figured into the equation. But the ultimate problem is that you and I and the whole world are in the dark. We do not perceive things as they really are. We do not yet know, *truly know,* who we are in Jesus Christ.

We have glimpsed it. It has flashed before us and kindled a twinkling of hope and faith and longing in us. But the real truth of what the Father has done with us and made of us in His Son is more like a rumor that we have heard and only vaguely believe.

We do not *know* as we are *known* (ICOR 13:12).

We are, as yet, only peeping out from under the table, like the children, beginning to suspect that perhaps the visitor may well be a friend and not an intruder. But the soul has not yet been utterly convinced.

When that happens, when the truth of what God has made of us in Jesus Christ, takes root in our souls and moves from being a hopeful suspicion to fundamental spiritual *knowledge,* then the glorious liberation of our adoption will become the spontaneous atmosphere of our lives and living, the light of our life. It will bear fruit in our thinking and seeing, in our relating and responding. It will express itself and ripple into every nook and cranny of our humanity and our human *being.* We will "become" what we "are" in Christ, reconciled, rightly related with the Father and with one another, and with creation.

As Jesus said, it is *knowing the truth* that sets us free (JN 8:31-32).

The transformation of our experience that we seek, Paul tells us, comes by the renewing of our mind, the conversion of our spiritual understanding, knowing and believing (ROM 12:2). Thus he prays for the Ephesians that God would grant to them the Spirit of wisdom and revelation in the knowledge of Christ, that the eyes of their heart would be enlightened, so that they would know the hope and riches and power of God's work in Christ (EPH 1:17-19; cf. 3:14-19; COL 1:9ff).

It all boils down to the spiritual knowledge of the soul.

That is the mission of the Holy Spirit now. He has been given to us to lead us to *know* what the Father has made of us in Jesus. And we are not speaking here of mere intellectual knowing, of some abstract doctrinal knowing. We are not speaking of mustard seed faith or hopeful suspicion, but of fully assured and convinced spiritual *knowledge*. Unassailable, in the Spirit, enlightened, unencumbered apprehension of the truth of who we are in Christ, in the depths of our souls, in the inner circle of our being, in the innermost man.

Meanwhile, the lack of *soul knowledge,* of what the Father has made of us in Jesus, does not leave us with neutral believing and knowing. It does not leave the soul, with all its spontaneous rippling and pervasive influence, sealed in a neutral vacuum. It leaves it under the harassment of Diabolos—the devil, the adversary, the accuser, the author of confusion, and the father of lies.

He constantly deceives us by declaring us to be lost, insecure, threatened, alone, and guilty. And his "word" creates the angst in our souls which drives us and forms itself into our being and relating. His word forms its own world and history.

The real problem is here; the glaring discrepancy between who we are in Christ and who we are in our experience is the result of profound spiritual deception—the lie of the evil one, on the one hand, and the soul's acceptance of his lie on the other.

The Ripple of the Soul's Deception

If we peeled back the layers of our humanity, all the way to our innermost being, what do you think we would find? I think we would find faith. That's right, *faith*. The problem for us is not that the soul is vacuous of faith. Every one of us is a believer. And we all live by our faith—our believing takes form; it expresses itself in our being. The problem is not whether we believe; the problem is *what* we believe.

The point that needs to be stressed here is that we have been deceived, sold a bill of goods about ourselves and God, and we believe it. Without exception we are all in the dark. Our spiritual seeing and believing is skewed. This means that what the soul perceives, what it knows and believes, is the lie that *I am lost*.

It may be, as we said earlier, that this spiritual believing has never crossed your conscious mind. It may be that you have never given it any thought. But remember, we are not speaking here of intellectual thought, we are speaking about the thinking of the soul. Whether we are aware of it consciously or not, we are all hearers and believers in the word of our lostness.

At the deepest level of your humanity, you *know* that you are lost. You know and believe that you are not right, not what you should be, fallen, alienated. You know that you are not home.

And that *knowledge* of the lie (which means a menacing sense of lostness) inescapably and irresistibly haunts us. It generates profound insecurity. It creates fear, hopelessness, and emptiness. And this knowledge alone, without adding other facets, such as guilt and shame, is lethal. For this mix ripples into all our living.

Insecurity, fear, hopelessness—and remember, we are not talking about surface level stuff here, we are talking about spiritual knowledge at the root of our being—spontaneously express themselves in attitudes; they take form in emotions, actions and reactions, and relationships.

For example, insecurity creates self-centeredness. It is automatic. It forces us into preoccupation with ourselves and our welfare. We have no choice but to protect ourselves—for *we* are not secure. It creates the feeling of loneliness, the need for acceptance, and the drive to prove ourselves to be "somebody." It goads us to find something that will make us secure. It just happens.

If only these were peripheral forces in our lives, things would not be so bad. But they are far too deep and personal to be superficial. They drive us. They dominate us. They form us. Our living, relating and responding, all become variations on the soul's zeal to cope with its intolerable insecurity.

We lust for power and control and position because the soul is desperately seeking security. And in the absence of knowledge of our security in Jesus Christ, the soul is forced to turn elsewhere to find security. It is forced to believe that these things will actually produce security for it.

Isn't the source of greed and the relentless lust for things simply a rippling expression of our soul's hunger for security? Doesn't greed come from believing that we will find real security when we have just a little more of whatever it is we think we need. "If I can just do this." "If I can just have one more." "If I can just move, or get this job, or get married, or become a member of that club, or get that car, or that degree, or that church." Or "if we can just get this program going in the church."

And then we become angry, frustrated, depressed, bitter and cynical, when we cannot get what we think will secure us, or we get it and it does not have the goods; it does not undo the angst. We become jealous of those who seem to have it and tear them down and slander them.

We prostrate ourselves before the club, or the *status quo,* or the look, for the barest and briefest hint at acceptance, or for the money. Bondage, sheer bondage!

Why? Why do we do this? Is it not because the soul is so desperately blinded, and therefore inconsolably menaced by lostness and insecurity, that it will do anything to make us feel as though we are *somebody?*

The whole process is insatiable. It never works. No matter how much we have, or how far we go, or how high we climb, or what we control, it does not work. We are still insecure little mice harassed and enslaved by every wind of *somebodiness.*

And the preacher tells us to do more for Jesus, read more, pray harder, get more involved in the church, give more money.

We have been deceived about ourselves and God. We are in the dark. On the one hand, the lie that we are lost, and its chief fruit of spiritual insecurity, is throwing us back upon ourselves. It is driving us—of all things—to believe in *ourselves* and in the fact that *we* can and must *do* something to make ourselves secure—to save ourselves and give ourselves life.

Our whole lives—our relationships, our acting and reacting, going and doing—begin to be simply the long ripple of the soul's sense of its lostness and thus the quest to save itself.

On the other hand, the lie, and its insecurity, is driving us into *denial,* which is the attempt to *ignore* the soul and its pain—for it is unbearable. We work with all our might to pretend that there is nothing wrong. There is no angst. We are fine.

We keep everything at the superficial level and steadfastly refuse to allow anything to awaken us or alert us to our pain. We make sure that we are busy, even busy at nothing. For to be still gets too close to the wavelength of the soul. We become wizards of rhetoric and hype, for we must convince ourselves and others that what we have is indeed *life.*

It is not to be forgotten that the most holy and religious people of Jesus' day—the Pharisees—were neither holy nor truly religious, but simply master practitioners of denial. They created the most sophisticated form of denial and they were not amateurs at their art. Yes, very often denial takes the form of religion, service to God.

Keep your eyes open, for the Pharisees teach us that it is more than possible for an entire system of religious service to God, a whole order of church life, to be nothing other than an ingenious work of pure denial—a mechanism of denial which craftily devises service to God, cheerfully dons the vestments and makes holy gestures, and uses the language of the gospel, as its chief means of keeping the cry and fear and pain of the soul from becoming the real and only question of life. Listen to what one of our veteran pastors says:

> People are uncomfortable with mystery (God) and mess (themselves). They avoid both mystery and mess by devising programs and hiring pastors to manage them.... We don't have to deal with ourselves or with God, but can use the vocabulary of religion and work in an environment that acknowledges God, and so be assured that we are doing something significant. (Eugene H. Peterson, *The Contemplative Pastor* [Grand Rapids: William B. Eerdmans Pub. Co., 1989], p. 48).

It is strange, but true, that the plethora of phone calls during the week, the self-imposed hectic schedules, the shuffling of children, the shopping spree, the hours of TV, the Friday night out with the guys, the ball game or fishing trip on Saturday, and church attendance, even preaching on Sunday, and the evangelistic blitz of Sunday afternoon can all be simply variations on the same theme of denial—coping with the soul and its insecurity with the drug of busyness.

The soul ripples. It forms itself spontaneously in human being and doing and relating. The one and only power that Satan has at his disposal is the power of illusion, lying. And his one strategy is to deceive us, to deceive our souls into believing that we are lost. For then he has us falling into one self-salvation scheme or one mode of denial after another.

The Hope of the Spirit

The fact remains, however, that God has reconciled the world in Jesus Christ. And the Father and Son are not silent about it in the least. Into the midst of our self-salvation schemes and our modes of denial, the Father, in the name of the vicarious man, showers the Spirit upon us. And the mission of the Spirit now is not to correct a few of the outer ripples—secondary and tertiary expressions of our soul's deception. He is not sent to us to put a Band-Aid over a spiritual cancer. He comes to cut a swath to our souls so that the Father can sound the Word of truth to us.

The Spirit has no interest in peripheral matters. He knows the real problem. And He comes to cut to the chase.

He is at work now, on and in all of us, doing surgery upon our eyes and ears that we may see the Light of Christ and hear the Word of Christ. He is striving with us and our profoundly darkened perception and believing to bring us to *know the truth* of what the Father has made of us in Christ.

That is the real solution—soul knowledge of who we are in Jesus, justified, reconciled, embraced and secured. And that is the essence of the Spirit's ministry now—revealing Jesus Christ to the deceived soul.

The Spirit doesn't trade in mere intellectual knowledge. He has come to teach the soul. He has come to disclose the knowledge of Jesus Christ to the inner recesses of our being. For the Spirit knows all about the ripple. He is a specialist in spiritual mechanics. He knows that *metanoia,* a great reversal, a conversion, of the perception of the soul, produces fruit.

Soul knowledge of the Father's embrace in Jesus creates its own person, life, relationships, world, and history. The Spirit knows that the glaring discrepancy, the fantastic breach, between "who we are in Jesus Christ" and "what we experience now" is caused by intense spiritual deception. He has thus come to bring light, the Light of life, the Word of life. He knows that the hearing of the Word of Christ in the soul begins to ripple security, peace, joy, glory, and healing, wholeness and right relationships into our experience. It begins to produce the kingdom in our lives, a river of living water flowing out of our innermost being.

It is not an accident that the apostle Paul calls it the fruit of the *Spirit* (GAL 5:22). Neither is it an accident that he says that the Spirit bears witness with our spirits that we are children of God, and cries out *Abba!* Father! in our hearts (ROM 8:15-16; GAL 4:6). For it is not our fruit. It is not our creation. It is the fruit of the witness of the Spirit to the truth in Christ as it reverberates in our souls—even as the glaring discrepancy is the ripple of the evil one's lie.

If you are like I am, then you want the Spirit to just get on with it. A little American instantaneous zapping will do quite well. "Flip the light switch, Holy Spirit, please." "Give us a secret formula or a magic elixir to take."

The Spirit is, in fact, getting on with it. That is what *this life* is all about. It is an 80 or so year spiritual enlightenment process. And that is what history is about—the enlightenment of the corporate soul of humanity, the education of the human race.

Somewhere along the way, I read of a scientific experiment carried out with newborn mice. The scientists took six mice, straight from the womb, and placed them in a specially designed little house. What was unique about this house was that it had no horizontal lines in it anywhere. Everything was either vertical or curved. For a whole year the mice lived in this house. They were never removed.

Then after a year, the scientists strung wires horizontally from one wall to the others—and they quickly discovered that the mice could not see them. The mice ran into the wires time and again, as if they were not there. They bloodied their little faces on the wires. They had no capacity to conceive of them. The scientists even painted the wires all the colors of the rainbow. But all for naught. The mice could not see them. Gradually, however, the mice developed the capacity to conceive of the wires.

This story is a vivid illustration of the problem of seeing. It shows us that perception, coming to see and know, is not instantaneous. It is a process. And just as importantly, it gives us a picture of the way that pain is involved in giving us eyes to see.

The whole of our lives comes down to this, being educated in the Spirit, being brought to perceive and *know* what the Father has made of us in Jesus Christ.

This knowing is a process that takes time and involves pain. It is even more so when the perception is spiritual and the knowing is that of the soul. And what complicates this process of coming to see is the fact that we have no *tabula rasa* (blank slate). Our seeing and knowing are already skewed, twisted, darkened—deceived. Moreover, we are inevitably part of a deceived cultural perception.

It is not a matter of zapping us. There are no instantaneous enlightenments of the soul—individually or corporately. It is a process. A long process, with pain and blood and sweat and tears. And that is what the Spirit is doing in our lives now, step by step, blow by blow, line by line.

In the gracious creativity of the Spirit, the deception and our failures are used as instruments of our enlightenment. As Luther said, "God makes theologians by sending them to hell." Misery is a good teacher. It teaches us that it is no friend, that we do not want to have fellowship with it, and it creates a hunger in us for real life. But this is not just the way God makes theologians. It is the way the Spirit educates us and the whole human race in the school of Christ.

He allows the deception of Diabolos to work within us, to form itself into our self-salvation schemes and into our various modes of denial. He gives us room—plenty of room—and time to try to make ourselves secure and give ourselves life. He gives us room to try to live in denial. He lets the lostness of our souls form into all sorts of brokenness.

The Spirit does not forsake us. He allows us and our families, our churches, cultures and nations and history, to get out of hand and fall apart. He allows the ripple to produce misery and nothingness and death in us. For He is using it all to bring us to the end of ourselves and our grandiose "life-producing" enterprises. He is using it to bring us to inescapable, piercing awareness of the lie's misery, where our own pain begins to shatter the facade and break through our denial. And we are in tears—individually, as families, churches and nations. And they are not superficial tears but tears of our innermost beings crying out for help and life.

This is how the Spirit cuts a swath to the soul. Listen to the words of John Newton, the author of *Amazing Grace* and other hymns.

> I asked the Lord, that I might grow
> In faith, and love, and every grace
> Might more of His salvation know,
> And seek more earnestly His face.
>
> I hoped that in some favored hour
> At once He'd answer my request,
> And by His love's constraining power
> Subdue my sins, and give me rest.

Instead of this, He made me feel
The hidden evils of my heart;
And let the angry powers of hell
Assault my soul in every part.

Yea more, with His own hand He seemed
Intent to aggravate my woe;
Crossed all the fair designs I schemed,
Blasted my gourds, and laid me low.

'Lord, why is this?' I trembling cried,
'Wilt thou pursue Thy worm to death?'
'Tis in this way,' the Lord replied,
'I answer prayer for grace and faith.

These inward trials I employ
From self and pride to set thee free;
And break thy schemes of earthly joy,
That thou may'st seek thy all in me.'

(from the hymn, *Prayer Answered by Crosses*)

It is this that makes sense out of the otherwise irrational admonition of the Scriptures to consider it all *joy* when all manner of trials come upon us (JMS 1:2) and to *glory*—not just accept, mind you, but *glory*—in our tribulations (ROM 5:3). It is all part of the Spirit's liberation.

He gathers up our failures, both as individuals and as families, churches and nations, and sharpens them into surgical instruments. He uses them to cut through our blindness and deception, so that we can begin to see and hear—really see and really hear—the shocking good news that has been there all along.

This is a divine world. Your life is not merely *your* life. Human history is not purely human. It is the history of the revelation of the vicarious man. It is the arena where the Spirit sovereignly strives with the deception and the broken disasters rippling from the souls of men and nations, and turns it all into a dynamic process of the education of the human race.

Under the tutelage of the Spirit, the news of what our Father, in sovereign grace, has made of us and done with us in Jesus Christ our Lord, reaches the trembling souls of men and nations which have been brought to misery by the deception. He strategically and surgically uses the deception to open our souls, and then He shines the Light of Jesus Christ into them. By the Word of God, He sounds our true hope and peace and liberation, our dignity and security and glory, into the inner recesses of our being. And we are ready to hear and see and believe. And hearing, seeing, believing ripple.

If we faint not, if we acknowledge our denial as it is being broken by pain, if we do not cling to our emptiness and religious nothingness as they are being exposed, if we do not resist the Spirit as He performs His surgery, *we* will *know* the truth and the truth will set *us* free.

If we do not love the darkness, the eternal Word of Jesus Christ will find its ready home in our *souls,* and the glorious reality of our adoption in Him will begin to ripple into every nook and cranny of our human existence. Our true humanity, hidden in Jesus Christ with His Father, shall begin to take form in our experience in the Spirit.

The news of the Triune God will fill our souls as peace, dignity, security and joy, hope, faith and love, and these will spontaneously express themselves in our working and playing, in our singing and dancing, in our plowing and fishing—in our living, responding and relating. And we will find ourselves becoming truly human and participating in the incarnate Son's life with His Father in the Spirit.

"For our momentary light affliction is producing in us an eternal weight of glory far beyond all comparison" (2COR 4:17).

"Beloved, now we are children of God, and it has not appeared as yet what we shall be. We know that, when He appears, we shall be like Him, because we shall *see Him* just as He is" (IJN 3:2).

O Hear the Word Declared to You
(to the tune Ellacombe)

O hear the Word declared to you as He became a man
    the Father's passion ceases not for His eternal plan
Wake up and see the time is full the great exchange has come
    the Son of God stands in our place the Father's will is done

O look and see the ancient Son though rich became so poor
    with our own poverty He fought and blow by blow endured
Wake up and see His painful wealth for this He came to be
    the treasure of the Triune Life in our humanity

O see our awful flesh embraced by Him who dwells on high
    He plunged into our darkness to bring the light of life
Wake up and see amazing grace in flesh the Father known
    to share with us within our reach the Life that is His own

O Spirit grant with unveiled face that we this Man would see
    and know His heart and soul and mind and share His victory
Inspire our empty hearts to run to this great vicarious One
    and give us fellowship with Him the Father's one true Son

© 1992 DR. C. BAXTER KRUGER

Dr. Kruger's latest book
The Great Dance
Now Available

The Great Dance is a masterpiece, an epic and astonishing vision of human life and the mystery of its intersection with the life of the Triune God.

Dr. Kruger charts a course from the Trinity to the incarnation to the union of humanity with God in Jesus Christ. In that light he offers a breathtaking interpretation of our human existence as participation in the life of the Father, Son and Spirit. He uncovers the untold dignity of our ordinary humanity--from motherhood to baseball, from relationships and music to golf, gardening and designing lakes. This is a book about who we are and why we are here and what is really happening in our lives.

Step by step, Dr. Kruger walks us through the stratagems of evil and the messes we make of our lives. More important, he explains why we hurt, what we are really after and how to get there, and why faith in Jesus Christ is so critical for abundant life.

The Great Dance is theology at its very best--steeped in tradition, yet unfamiliar and exciting, even revolutionary; deeply personal and honest, yet universally relevant. Written with pace and poetry and winsome grace, *The Great Dance* is the voice of the ancient church speaking to us across the ages through the pen of a Southerner who loves *life.*

The Great Dance

The Christian Vision Revisited

C. Baxter Kruger, Ph. D.

PERICHORESIS PRESS
P. O. Box 98157 • Jackson, MS 39298
(601) 919-1959

"Baxter Kruger has done a great service for all Christians who are trying to put wheels on the meaning of the Trinity for their everyday lives. His down-home storytelling and energetic, lyrical prose combine to pull our hearts and very beings into 'the great dance' of life. On first reading one of Baxter's books I cried out, 'This is it!' He put flesh on my bony understanding of how our triune God loves me in and through my daily, frequently misshaped, living. And now *The Great Dance* takes me further, presenting me with the wonderful scene of my everyday existence taken up, through Christ's ascension, into the very life of God. I commend this book to anyone who longs to experience meaning, purpose, and joy in everyday duties and pleasures."

W. J. Douglas Ball
Mississauga, Ontario, Canada

Order Form For
PERICHORESIS BOOKS AND TAPES

Books by C. Baxter Kruger, Ph. D.

___ *The Great Dance* ($12) .... $ _____

___ *The Secret* ($6) .... $ _____

___ *HOME* ($6) .... $ _____

___ *God Is For Us* ($9)... $ _____

___ *The Parable of the Dancing God* ($2) .... $ _____

Perichoresis Tape Series

____ "The Nicene Creed"
   Dr. C. Baxter Kruger
   Dr. Robert Lucas (set of 4 @ $20) .... $ _____

___ "Prayer and the Triune God of Grace"
   Prof. James B. Torrance (set of 4 @ $20)...................... $ _____

___ "The Secret of Narnia: Light from C.S. Lewis"
   Upshaw, Stockett and Kruger (set of 4 @ $20)........... $ _____

___ "The Great Dance: The Christian Vision Revisited"
   Dr. C. Baxter Kruger (set of 4 @ $20)........................... $ _____

___ Perichoresis Tape of the Month ($100) .... $ _____

SHIPPING AND HANDLING	Sub Total	$ _____
1 - 8 books $3	Postage	$ _____
9 - 20 books $5	**TOTAL**	$ _____

TO ORDER
Make checks payable to: Perichoresis
Mail order and check to:
   Perichoresis • P. O. Box 98157 • Jackson, MS 39298

Name_____

Address _____

City _____State _____ Zip_____

PLEASE PRINT CLEARLY

Phone (601) 919-1959
www.perichoresis.org • email: cbkruger@netdoor.com